Sheffield Hallam University
Learning and IT Services
Collegiate Learning Centre
Collegiate Crescent Campus
Sheffield   S10 2BP

101 888 138 7

Sheffield Hallam University
Learning and Information Service
Withdrawn From Stock

KT-197-267

ONE WEEK LOAN

– 2 OCT 2009

17 OCT 2012

HATE ON THE NET

Advances in Criminology

Series Editor: David Nelken

The full list of series titles can be found at the back of the book

Hate on the Net
Extremist Sites, Neo-fascism On-line, Electronic Jihad

ANTONIO ROVERSI
University of Bologna, Italy

L'Odio in Rete, translated by
LAWRENCE SMITH

ASHGATE

© Società editrice Il Mulino, Bologna 2006; this version 2008
Translated by Lawrence Smith

All rights reserved. No part of this publication may be reproduced, stored in a retrieval system or transmitted in any form or by any means, electronic, mechanical, photocopying, recording or otherwise without the prior permission of the publisher.

Some of the content of this book refers to text taken from websites which may have changed since the time of writing. Ashgate accepts no responsibility for this content, its accuracy or the views and opinions, including those of the author, expressed within this book.

Published by
Ashgate Publishing Limited
Gower House
Croft Road
Aldershot
Hampshire GU11 3HR
England

Ashgate Publishing Company
Suite 420
101 Cherry Street
Burlington, VT 05401-4405
USA

Ashgate website: http://www.ashgate.com

The translation of this book has been funded by SEPS – Segretariato Europeo per le Pubblicazioni Scientifiche.
SEPS – Segretariato Europeo per le Pubblicazioni Scientifiche
Via Val d'Aposa 7
40123 Bologna
Italy
Email: seps@alma.unibo.it

www.seps.it

British Library Cataloguing in Publication Data
Roversi, Antonio
   Hate on the Net : extremist sites, neo-fascism on-line,
   electronic jihad. - (Advances in criminology)
   1. Hate crimes 2. Hate groups - Computer network resources
   3. Right-wing extremists - Computer network resources
   4. Terrorism - Computer network resources 5. Web sites
   I. Title
   364.1

Library of Congress Cataloging in Publication Data
Roversi, Antonio.
 Hate on the net : extremist sites, neo-fascism on-line, electronic jihad / by Antonio Roversi.
   p. cm. -- (Advances in criminology)
 Includes bibliographical references and index.
 ISBN 978-0-7546-7214-2
 1. Racism--Computer network resources. 2. Race discrimination--Computer network resources. 3. Antisemitism--Computer network resources. 4. Internet. 5. World Wide Web. 6. Cyberspace--Social aspects. 7. Technology--Social aspects. I. Title.

 HT1521.R69 2008
 025.06'3058--dc22

2007034132

 ISBN 978-0-7546-7214-2

Printed and bound in Great Britain by MPG Books Ltd, Bodmin, Cornwall.

Contents

Publisher's Note

Some of the content of this book refers to text taken from websites which may have changed since the time of writing. Ashgate accepts no responsibility for this content, its accuracy or the views and opinions, including those of the author, expressed within this book.

In addition, a few further points of clarification have come to light since the work was translated.

On p. 4 the author states that he will not be using the terms 'terrorist' or 'terrorism' thereafter. These terms do appear later in the book where the author cites others' use of them or where they are set terms.

Since translation of the work it has come to the publisher's attention that the Hagannah website, as referred to on p. 7, states that the founder is supported in its running by a group of volunteers. It is unknown when this information became available and if the author was aware of it.

The author dates the founding of Rimini Forza Nuova as 1997. An alternative source dates this 1999.

On p. 49 the author refers to 'Celtic crosses'. These are the characteristic Celtic crosses or sunwheels associated with right-wing groups in Italy.

General Editor's Preface

When I proposed to my friend and colleague Antonio Roversi the idea of translating this book for the Ashgate series of 'Advances in Criminology' I had no intimation that this would also become his testament. In the last few months of his life, still only middle aged, he used what remained of his energies to help ensure that his work would reach a wider audience. This was something that mattered more to him here than it had for his other writings, even though many of these too have reached an international audience. In this introduction I will say just a few words about the author and his book which may help to explain why this was so.

Antonio was one of the most creative and versatile of Italian sociologists. He wrote authoritatively about social theorists such as Max Weber and Norbert Elias, carried out trail breaking first-hand ethnographic investigations of 'hooligan' football supporters and extreme right wing groups, and pioneered studies of the sociology of the Internet. As a person, Antonio's erudition was rarely put on display. What was more obvious was his playful intellectual curiosity and an often ironic approach to life (something which emerges from the first pages of the book). Few people knew that he combined this unusual lightness of being with exemplary civil courage and integrity (which also characterises the life of his father, one of Italy's foremost contemporary poets). As the temporary block on Antonio's academic career showed, he was willing to pay the price that such independence usually entails. As I see it therefore, it is this side of his character that helps explain the importance of this book for him. Reading through the websites of these extremists groups gave him a sense of urgency about the need to point out the 'darker side of the net'. During his research he suffered frequent nightmares, and its publication also generated a number of threats. But what frightened him most was the cruel side of human nature that he had discovered, not his own danger.

But why is this book in a series about criminology? There are certainly relevant implications in what Antonio has to tell us about the Internet as a tool for crime, whether these concern the organisation of football hooliganism, the extremes of 'hate speech', or, more generally, the definition and regulation of non-state terrorism (state terrorism usually relies on less public channels). He has salient things to tell us about the creation of 'suitable enemies' and about the function of communication about deviant misbehaviour in maintaining the boundaries of groups rather than passing on information.

But his overall concern is with the growth of open legitimation of violence, and the consequent threat of yet another reversal in what Elias described as the 'the civilizing process'. If criminology is not interested in these themes what claim can it have on our attention?

Antonio does not offer us easy answers. Despite having become an expert in the field of computer-mediated communication he raises but does not resolve (as how could he?) the issues of the technical possibility and the moral advisability of some form of censorship. Nor is he unaware that he focuses on only one part of a larger picture. He is careful, for example, not to use the word 'terrorism', and makes reference more than once to the way democratic states sometimes manipulate the shocking communications of their adversaries so as to serve their own military purposes. His complaint about websites which advocate jihad in its most bloody form is not that this shows that 'our' culture is superior to 'theirs': rather it is that such sites do less than justice to the contributions of Islamic culture itself. He wants the net to host free and fierce debate about values, to encourage the force of argument, not the language of force.

This translation,[1] carefully prepared by Lawrence Smith, makes all too clear the potential for harm of the new means of communication on which we all increasingly depend. Whatever the once fond hopes of building a better world in cyberspace, and its still abundant possibilities, the net is increasingly being shaped by the needs of profit making, pornography – and propaganda. An instrument for encouraging global communication in more ways than could ever have been foreseen is being hijacked in an attempt to 'Balkanise' users into non-communicating tribes. A technology that permits experimentation with different selves becomes a tool for enforcing fixed and ineluctable identities. A virtual medium, in which the imagination can take flight, turns into a repository of instructions for the creation of bombs. At its worst, as the author writes, 'the Internet has become a means by which old resentments draw new breath, contempt for the other is manifested in all its virulence, hate for who is on the other side is screamed with words dripping in blood, and the desire to settle old scores is exhibited brandishing the most menacing of symbols'. In his view, if the world is to become a safer place, all sides have to learn to find other ways to face up to conflicts of values (and the competition for resources that often lie behind them). I know that Stefania and Caterina, Antonio's family, hope that this book may make a contribution, however small, to this goal.

David Nelken

---

1   This translation was made possible with the kind financial assistance of SEPS.

Introduction

I did all the research for this book sitting comfortably in my study. All I had need of was a laptop, an always-on connection to the Internet and a lot of time for navigating between the infinite pages of the web. Nothing else. And, of course, the intention of studying the websites of the Italian Ultras, of fascist and neo-Nazi organizations (both those in Italy and in other countries) and of armed Middle-Eastern groups, in other words, the websites of those who have made hate and the exaltation of violence – and even killing and extermination – the main content of their presence on the web. How can this sort of research be defined? Sociologists distinguish between 'desk' and 'field' studies. 'Desk' studies involve the analysis of statistical data that has been collected in various ways: through questionnaires, time series and sampling. In the case of 'field' studies, instead of being required to interpret the significance of tables of figures, the researcher is supposed to personally enter the environment of a group or a certain area of a city, observe what happens around him and question those who enter within his field of study. Given this classification, I wasn't sure which category my research belonged to. I sat the whole time at a desk but I didn't analyse any statistics. Broadly speaking I did enter the worlds of certain groups, but I never asked questions of anyone. In practice all I did was to look at clusters of pixels coming together to compose images which appeared on my computer screen. And I tried to understand what those images were intended to communicate. On the assumption that some human agency lay behind them, and that they were not merely the product of what in technical terms is called the 'rendering' of HTML code, or of the execution of a piece of JavaScript, but the transposition via the Internet of the feelings, points of view and convictions of real men and women. Some of whom are living among us, perhaps just a few doors away: they dress like us, eat what we eat, watch what we watch and, in the case of the Ultras, share the same passions as many of us. Some live in far distant countries and are very different from us in how they live and think. Yet, near or distant as the case may be, these men and women have something in common. Something which they communicate to us using that strange plastic box filled with electronic circuits with its glass screen which we call a computer, which enables them to construct their messages and publish them on the web. And that is why I didn't need much in the way of the equipment that is typical of my profession to carry out my research.

What I realized almost at once was that the Internet was crawling with the kind of sites I wanted to study. Some were easy to get to, others less so, though they were not exactly hidden. All that was necessary to find them was a bit of patience and perseverance. Sometimes addresses were provided by those who hosted such sites on their server – as in the case of many Ultra groups. Sometimes they were provided by those who monitor the web in pursuit of anti-Semitic or terrorist groups around the world: state agencies or organizations which appear to be private and which will be mentioned in the following chapters. The second thing that I came to realize immediately was that each of these sites, which we can call 'hate sites' for obvious reasons, addresses a public of faithful readers. It is sometimes easy to deduce who their audiences are, but how numerous they are is more problematic, though my impression is that they attract substantial numbers of visitors. Not merely visitors who are curious, but people who identify with the messages of hate and violence that these sites disseminate untiringly every day, by means of the Internet.

But why have I chosen to study this matter? At the end of the day the answer is a simple one. Generally speaking, research is motivated, before all else, by curiosity and the desire to learn something new. In my case I was doubly curious. On the one hand, I wanted to see how the groups of Ultras, fascists and neo-fascists on whom I had carried out ethnographic research in the nineties, before the Internet had become a mass technology, were using the Internet.[1] On the other, I was struck by the ease and efficacy with which some armed Middle-Eastern groups were using the Internet to communicate and propagate their ideas. That is to say, shortly after September 11. I am old enough to remember the Italian terrorism of the '70s and '80s – the Red Brigades and the other armed groups of the extreme left and right – killing someone almost every day. Those groups, too, issued communiqués and distributed manifestos. But all their material was produced using a typewriter and a duplicating machine. After every terrorist action they left a communiqué in a rubbish bin or a telephone box. Then they telephoned a newspaper to say where it was hidden. A journalist went along to get it, and the next day we could read about it in the newspaper, or hear it summarized on the evening news. And if my memory does not deceive me, there were only a couple of audio documents in that period. The phone calls that Valerio Morucci made to Aldo Moro's wife and to his assistant, first to urge the intervention of the Italian political parties and then to communicate that he had been killed and that his body was in the boot of a red Renault in

---

1   Roversi, A. (1992), *Calcio, tifo e violenza. Il teppismo calcistico in Italia* (Bologna: Il Mulino); Roversi, A. (1995), 'I naziskin italiani. Studio di un caso', *Polis*, **3**; Roversi, A. (1999), 'Giovani di destra e giovani di estrema destra', *Rassegna Italiana di Sociologia*, **4**.

Via Caetani. But these audio documents were the fruit of telephone tapping carried out by the police.

That was back then. Now things happen differently. During the 'Years of Lead',[2] did anyone ever see the face of a brigatista, or read the whole of one of their communiqués, or hear one of them, in an hour long speech, claim to have reason on their side? No. Their faces, when we saw them, were faded copies of photographs taken years before. Everything else was filtered and condensed for us by articles in newspapers and news programmes. But today with a simple click of your mouse you can leap over intermediary agencies and see and hear bin Laden in person while he makes an appeal to the American people, or an Afghan commander explaining step by step how to construct an explosive belt with which to blow up yourself and those around you in a public place, or read the complete statement which claimed responsibility for the London bombings.

It was the combination of these different stimuli that spurred me to begin this research. It was the desire to see, hear and read – to find out for myself, in other words – what those who were, for various reasons, on the other side, had and have to say. People I have known and people I will never know. A curiosity that was triggered by an episode that I relate in the first chapter. Because this book is not just an account of a piece of research and its results. It is also the story of how this research unfolded over time. I am well aware that I should have followed the rigid rules of scientific publication. Use the first person plural; limit myself to the exposition of data, facts, theories, interpretations and so on. But I haven't done so. And I haven't done so because I wasn't able to do it. Research is always also a personal experience, however dry and aseptic its object, and even if, as in my case, it is conducted comfortably seated in front of a computer in one's own study. It is difficult to remain completely detached when confronted with certain 'messages', whether they be text, audio or visual. And I'm not referring only to the images of the lynchings of 'niggers' of which American neo-Nazi sites are full, to the anti-Semitic jokes on certain Italian sites or to the ashen, lifeless face of Enzo Baldoni which suddenly appeared while I was visiting a Middle-Eastern site. I'm referring also to the songs for Palestinian children, to accounts of punitive actions by Blackshirts, to the pure filth of certain Ultra webpages – of which I will attempt provide an account in the following chapters. Faced with this discharge of obscenity, cruelty, hate and total lack of respect for human dignity, this appetite for violence and this contempt for the life and opinions of others, I confess that I was often tempted by the desire to switch off the computer and move on to something else. And it made me realise that

---

2 The 'Years of Lead' ('anni di piombo') refers to the Italy of the 1970s and early 1980s, a period characterized by widespread social conflicts and terrorist acts carried out by extra-parliamentary movements.

I would never manage give an account of my experience in the course of this research with the detachment that is required of a scientific investigation. I say this to warn my readers that they will also find, dispersed in the following chapters, personal recollections, feelings and reflections which I hope will not cause annoyance.

In any case, the reader will judge the value and quality of my work. And with this foregone conclusion I could end this brief introduction. However, I feel that I should make two further clarifications, or rather provide answers to two possible and foreseeable objections. The first could be of this order: why have I not also analysed sites of extreme left or radical left provenance? The answer is simple: because I have found very few. Apart from that cited on the first page of the next chapter, which was in any case more of an archive of historical documents easily obtainable elsewhere, I found only two: that of the Irish Republican Army (which, however, appears not to have been updated since 28 August 1998),[3] and that of the Red and Anarchist Action Network.[4] Too little to permit an analysis which would allow generalization. At most, in my view, they permit research of the case study kind. And naturally, it goes without saying that if some other researcher proves more capable than me in finding extreme left or radical left websites secreted in hidden corners of the web I will be more than happy to integrate his or her findings with my own. The second objection which I wish to forestall concerns the fact that from this point onwards I do not use the term 'terrorist' or 'terrorists' but substitute instead the expression 'armed Middle-Eastern groups' or sometimes an expression employed by Ulrich Beck in one of his essays: 'groups which have individualized war'. The reason, in this case too, is simple, and for a sociologist, inevitable. The term 'terrorist' is clearly a term which includes a value judgement on the part of the user and which may not be accepted by those to whom it is applied or by third parties. If I call a member of an Ultra group an 'Ultra' he certainly will not object, indeed he will probably be proud to be known as such. If I call a person a fascist who openly proclaims himself as such, has no hesitation in eulogizing Benito Mussolini and sees the fascist epoch as the most glorious in Italian history, I do nothing more than give him a name with which he already identifies himself. The same thing is not true, however, for the Middle-Eastern 'terrorist'. Whatever my personal opinions on the matter, the fact remains that some see him as a murderer of innocents and others – like it or not – as a freedom fighter. And it is only for this reason that I have preferred to have recourse to a terminology that is neutral such as that which I have indicated above.

At this point nothing remains but to invite my reader to turn the page.

---

3   Available at http://www.geocities.com/CapitolHill/Congress/2435 [Accessed 25 June 2007 (translator)].

4   Now mirrored at http://raan.fightcapitalism.net/www.redanarchist.org [Accessed 25 June 2007 (translator)].

Chapter 1

The Net and the Web:
Web Communication

1. The dark side of the web

For a moment I thought that I was seeing things. Then that it must be a joke. But the webpage that had appeared on my computer was undoubtedly that of the Red Brigades. Or at least it was closely associated with them. It looked like one of their communiqués. One of those communiqués they used to produce on a duplicating machine. The heading 'BRIGATE [five pointed star] ROSSE' stood out in the centre. A little bit below, the subheading 'Facts, Documents and People'. Perhaps because of my bewilderment at finding myself in front of that webpage, I remember what struck me most was the copyright notice, '© Brigate Rosse 2001–2004', clearly visible at the bottom. I had a momentary flash of brigatisti demonstrating in the street with placards bearing the slogan 'Viva private property!'

I'm not joking. That page, or rather that website,[1] really existed. And it's still there right now, while I'm writing this. All you need to do to check it out is to type www.brigaterosse.it[2] in your browser. I can't now say how I came across that page. Perhaps I had clicked on some link or I had done some research on Google. What is certain is that it was a case of serendipity, a chance but valuable discovery (I already had the project of writing a book like this in mind), which placed me in front of precisely what I was looking for. Or at least a part of it.

In much the same way I came across the websites of Middle-Eastern armed groups. One day I set out to find computer games in flash format. Flash is fantastic. In terms of image quality, fluidity and speed it is almost on a par with video games. And on the web you can find lots of material created using this technology. If you find a file which is called – for example – race.swf, you can be ninety per cent sure that once you have launched it you will be able to race on a Formula One circuit at the wheel of a Ferrari. And that if the file is called pingpong.swf, once downloaded and installed on your computer,

---

1   By website I mean a collection of interconnected webpages hosted on a server. A website always has a unique address – called a URL – of the type: www.name_of_site.com (or .org, .it, etc.), by means of which it is possible to reach the site via computer.

2   Accessed by translator 26 June 2007.

you will be able to challenge a Japanese champion with smashes and low balls. In short, I was looking for something of the kind when, in a forest of .swf files with names which were more or less explicit, there appeared one with an odd tag: mal7.swf. Curious, I downloaded it and inserted it into a webpage which I had set up to play my flash games and opened it in my browser. Another surprise. First a black screen came up which slowly filled with phrases written in Arabic while in the background a voice sang what seemed to my ears some sort of repeated litany. After some moments the inside of a cockpit appeared in a plane heading towards the Twin Towers in New York. Then came those images – shown on televisions the world over – of the two planes crashing into the Twin Towers. After a few moments the picture changed. The centre of the screen was now occupied by a still of the two towers in flames while images of the hijackers who had seized those planes and who had died in the impact began to scroll upwards on the right of the screen accompanied by the voice of bin Laden making a speech in Arabic. Bin Laden must have spoken for a minute or two before the screen went black again and the text in Arabic reappeared. It didn't take a genius to realize what I had downloaded from the web. I had downloaded a video – in flash format – in which some Middle-Eastern Islamic group claimed responsibility for 9/11. The file, as I have said, was called 'mal7.swf'.

More or less in the same period, in March 2004, four Italians were seized in Iraq. Security contractors working for a private company, as the newspapers discretely put it. Their names were Umberto Cupertino, Salvatore Stefio, Maurizio Agliana and Fabrizio Quattrocchi. The latter, as is well known, was brutally killed by his kidnappers a few days later. A video-tape of his death was sent to the Arabic television station *Al Jazeera* which refused to show it because it was too gruesome. A sensibility and a respect with regard to the death of a civilian which was not shown a month later when a young American by the name of Nick Berg was kidnapped. Nick Berg was killed, or rather, decapitated, on 11 May 2004 and the video of his execution was rapidly diffused worldwide. The story of this young American Jew was a strange one. Already under investigation by American security forces in 2001 after the attack on the Twin Towers for having given the only Arab arrested in the US for that crime – Zacarias Moussaoui – access to his email account and password, he went around alone, in the Iraq of those times, without knowing a word of Arabic, in search of some Arab who wanted to install a television antenna on the roof of his house. And the way in which the video was found and circulated was also strange.

The video of the killing of Nick Berg was in fact discovered by the person responsible for maintaining the Haganah website.[3] What is the

---

3   Available at http://internet-haganah.co.il/haganah/ [Accessed 25 June 2007 (translator)].

Haganah website? An Israeli site run by someone who answers to the name of Aaron Weisburd, who lives in America. The Haganah site is a bit out of the ordinary for a number of reasons. Above all, it has a frequently updated database of all Middle-Eastern terrorist websites. And the sites it manages to monitor number several hundreds – as can be confirmed by consulting its database. It's difficult to believe that one man could run such a big operation, though the site says he is helped by volunteers. In all probability, a group of some kind is involved. It is still more difficult to believe that work as sensitive as this has been left in private hands without some authority – for want of a better expression – sticking its nose in. In the second place, the announcement that the video had been found was posted on this site with a message dated 11 May, time: 15.36. Its source was given – the website Al Ansar – together with the web address[4] of the same, and the video was put on the Haganah web server. In a message posted the following day – 12 May – it was stated that 'regarding the movie, we hosted it on a couple of our sites, and were rewarded with a denial-of-service attack. Most of our mirrors are still up and running, but not all of them, and I've had to remove the movie'. A denial-of-service attack is a strategy used by someone, more usually a group, whose object is to crash a server. Nothing was said about who was responsible – something that it is difficult to determine – but presumably the perpetrators of the DoS were hackers of the Islamic faith.[5] In any case, the video disappeared from the Haganah site. The Al Ansar site, on the other hand, was still functional and accessible, even if exasperatingly slow. In fact, I managed to connect and take a screenshot,[6] but I couldn't find the video.

I then learnt, again from the Haganah site, that 'Like us, they also were hosting the movie for a time, but they have since removed it from circulation. It's a difficult movie to host, for a number of reasons'. That 'they' referred to a website by the name of Evote.com which was still providing online access to the video, which, it claimed, 'was provided to Evote.com by Aaron Weisburd, Director of Internet Haganah'. So it seems that same Weisburd, who had already published the video on his own server, was apparently also responsible for its distribution.

I don't know – I have to admit – what sort of reputation Evote.com[7] has, but the fact remains that the video also appeared shortly afterwards on one of

---

4   Last known address: http://al-ansar.biz/vb/.

5   Who in fact have a site (last known address: http://alqa3edah.i6networks.com/hack. html) where it is possible to find a programme – Evil Team – that can be used to crash a server with a denial-of-service attack.

6   A screenshot is a photograph of what is on the screen of a computer. In this case the Al Ansar site as it appeared in my browser.

7   Available at http://www.evote.com/homepage/new_homepage.asp [Accessed 25 June 2007 (translator)].

the most nauseating sites on the Internet: Ogrish.com.[8] This is a site which usually hosts videos of amputations, rapes, homicides and pleasant things of that nature. The news that Ogrish was hosting the video must have got about quickly because when I accessed the site I found this text on the homepage: 'We are currently experiencing a huge amount of traffic. And Yes we have the video of the beheading of the American civilian (Nicholas Berg) in Iraq. – DOWNLOAD HERE – (Right Click, then Save Target As). Just like all the other uncensored videos and images previously posted, we feel that it's important to show what the human race is capable of in all its uncensored form. We don't MAKE you watch the footage; we just give you the choice. This is the world we're living in right now, sad but true ... Can you handle life?'. I learnt of the existence of this site and of the fact that it was hosting the video because that same day I had launched a file sharing programme[9] and on entering 'Iraq', I had found the video of the killing of Nick Berg, in the Ogrish version, in pride of place on the list. The people offering it were numbered in hundreds. I had already downloaded the file. It was 10.2Mb. The video also appeared on another site called Tides World Press Reports together with an English translation of what Nick Berg's executioner said before decapitating him.[10]

At that point I asked myself: how had newspapers and television stations the world over already managed to get hold of the video on 11 May? In my view there were two possibilities: either that newspapers and television stations around the world were permanently linked to the Haganah site, had read the message when it appeared and had managed to download it before the Al Ansar site went off-line, or the Haganah site itself had been responsible for its diffusion. In this case, in fact, we were not dealing with a video delivered to *Al Jazeera* or some other Arabic television station. The video had been available only on the Al Ansar site, a site known only to intelligence experts. Why was it distributed? An ingenuous question, but a legitimate one, given that the video of the killing of Fabrizio Quattrocchi, which could not have been any less horrific, had not been. The ulterior motive that I came up with then, and which I still suspect could be the explanation, is this: it was a damage control response to the controversy concerning torture in Abu Ghraib prison and also perhaps to the fact – in the event, ignored by the media – that on that very same day the Taguba report was delivered

---

8   The website was incorporated into LiveLeak.com on 31 October 2006 which is available at http://www.liveleak.com/ (translator's note). I would discourage anyone of any sensitivity, especially of any moral sensibility, from viewing this site.

9   A file sharing programme is used for finding or sharing files between private users. It is mainly used to share music files in MP3 format.

10 The site has since disappeared. Its known address was http://tides.cambridge.org/ Translations/Berg.htm (translator's note).

to Congress and its results were made public. This was a report drawn up by the American general responsible for the investigation commissioned the previous January into allegations that suspected Iraqi terrorists were being tortured in American prisons in Iraq.

My journey into the world of Middle-Eastern sites had begun. I didn't yet know exactly what to look for or where to find it – above all I didn't yet know what I would find myself seeing and hearing – but at the time carrying out research on this new phenomenon, the web used as a means of planetary communication by groups of Islamic combatants, seemed to be the natural continuation and completion of various investigations that I had undertaken in the past. About twenty years before I had in fact carried out research into the world of football Ultras. Following that I had conducted research on a group of young people of the extreme right – or 'naziskin', as they were then called in Italy. The material I collected served me for a number of books and several essays. When, years later, I found myself in the position of writing a manual on communication via computer, the idea of including a chapter on the way in which these groups used the Internet for the transmission of their messages of hate and violence came spontaneously to me. On that occasion I based myself on material I had collected and selected in order to integrate *ex post* my knowledge of these two phenomena. As far as the Ultras were concerned the matter was simple. I created a webpage with links to all the groups which, as far as I knew, had their own website and every so often I accessed them to check for new developments. I drew on two principal sources in the case of fascist and neo-Nazi sites: a well documented research study by Enrica Cavina,[11] and reports produced by the Simon Wiesenthal Centre[12] which publishes a CD-ROM every year of the sites of far-right groups around the world and estimates that there about 40,000 of them. An estimate which seems excessively high to me but which, given the authority of the source, I hesitate to challenge. Why do I think it too high? Because of the fact that a large number of these sites were abandoned by their creators while still under construction and are consequently rather poor in terms of content, and because of the fact that an equally large number of them tend to disappear after a certain time. They are hosted on servers which provide space free of charge to those who want to create a website but as soon as the provider becomes aware of their characteristics they are often closed down and disappear without a trace.

This does not alter the fact that the web is full of what Enrica Cavina calls 'Black Pages'. What they are like, what they contain and what types of

---

11 Cavina, E. (2001), Le Pagine Nere. Informazione e comunicazione nel mondo unificato del Web, *Le Nuove Destre Movimento radicali in Europa, Atti del Convegno di Studi, Istituto Storico della Resistenza e dell'Età Contemporanea in Ravenna e Provincia.*

12 Available at http://www.wiesenthal.com.

messages they transmit over the Internet are things that I hope to document
to the reader's satisfaction in the chapter dedicated to them. Here I'll limit
myself to providing a foretaste of the many surprises I found myself facing in
the course of my research into the Black Pages. Only two examples. There's
an American website that calls itself White Aryan Resistance.[13] Among the
many things it offers its visitors are a few games. Here is a small selection:

File Name: KZ Manager Millennium
Description: Manager of Concentration Camp

File Name: Rattenjagt
Description: Kill the Jewish rats!

File Name: Nigger Hunt
Description: Safari in Africa – Kill all the Niggers you can!

That should be enough to give you an idea. The second example concerns a
website that is not strictly speaking fascist or neo-Nazi. It goes by the name
of Holy War, it has versions in both Italian and English and I would define
it as a rather 'traditional' website as most of its pages are dedicated to a re-
evaluation of pre-conciliar Catholicism. It is a receptacle for anti-modernism
and anti-semitism. It became famous for, *inter alia*, being closed down
more than once by the judicial authorities because, among the abominations
it contains and which I will illustrate, there was one that was particularly
alarming: a complete list of all Italian families of Jewish origin. A list that is
to be found at the end of a series of anti-Semitic attacks of a virulence that it
is difficult to imagine and organized by theme in different sections: 'St. John
Chrysostom's homilies against the Jews', 'St Augustine's Treatise against
the Jews', 'Jewish Lies', 'The Diary of Anne Frank (a sensational fake)',
'Falsified proof of the Holocaust in Jewish Propaganda', 'Saints eliminated
by the Racist Jewish Mafia', and so on. Despite being repeatedly closed
down, Holy War is still alive and kicking. As far as I am aware, it is hosted
on a Norwegian server.[14]

Of this site I will have more to say in the third chapter. I won't be
saying anything, however, about another site whose name and web address
I deliberately withhold for reasons which will be clear in a moment. First
I would like to recall a phrase from a book by Kevin Mitnick, in which
he affirms that there are things on the web that shouldn't be there and,

---

13 Available at http://www.resist.com/home.htm [Accessed 25 June 2007 (translator)].

14 The site has since disappeared. Its known address was http://holywar.com (translator's
note).

above all, there are things in places where they shouldn't be.[15] This phrase came to mind when I visited the website of the US Justice Department and found the Al Qa'ida military training manual.[16] On looking more closely, though, I discovered that it was a bowdlerized version, from which the more sensitive passages had been expurgated. 'The Department is only providing the following selected text from the manual because it does not want to aid in educating terrorists or encourage further acts of terrorism'. But, I said to myself reading that notice, perhaps an integral version of the manual is available somewhere else. I wasn't wrong. All I needed to do was use Google and here was a site where the manual – of whose existence I hadn't been previously aware – was available in all its integral glory. And that was not all. The manual was contained in a section of the site – a section called 'Files' – that, as proclaimed in a warning, was 'for terroristic purposes only'. And, in fact, in a subsection, I found material of this kind: *Bombs/Explosives/ Experiments How can I Train Myself for the Jihad?* (the Al Qa'ida manual), the famous *The Terrorist's Handbook*, and even *The Unabomb Guide to Blowing up Universities*, together with other instructive texts like *Basic Explosives and Weekend Violence: How to Have Fun When You're Bored Out of Your Skull* in which, amongst other things, there is a detailed explanation of how to shoot people as they drive by in a car. All this, I repeat, within reach of a simple search using Google.

I could list other sites and other materials that I found in the preliminary phases of my research on what I call the dark side of the web. Dark not because hidden in some secret or inaccessible corner. On the contrary. As I think you have already realized, all that is necessary is a bit of patience, a good search engine, what Norbert Elias calls 'a low disgust threshold', and Bob's your uncle. You can find these sites quite easily. I call it the dark side because it is populated with individuals and groups who all use, though with differing accents and idioms – with some rare but important exceptions – the language of violence, of bullying and annihilation with regard to some of their fellow human beings. Behind these webpages there are men and women who feed an ancient predisposition for hatred that we thought had been uprooted by the development of civilization or that had at least been relegated to some inoffensive and nostalgic niche of our planet, but which here, on the contrary, reappears with an intensity that is in some ways surprising. It is a sentiment that uses the most modern of our means of communication and the most advanced of available technologies in order

---

15 Kevin Mitnick is considered to be one of the most talented computer hackers in the world. He was hunted as a criminal by the FBI and served a long sentence after his arrest. Today he works as a security consultant for a number of American firms. The quote comes from his book *The Art of Deception* (Indianapolis: Wiley, 2002).

16 Available at http://www.usdoj.gov/ag/trainingmanual.htm.

to manifest itself. With success, it must be admitted, though in certain cases it only achieves its object through the use of some stratagem. And it is a sentiment which, as the Internet and the WWW show, is not confined to a particular category of people; it does not flourish only in a highly specific social and economic context: on the contrary, it is present in many corners of our planet in a way that clearly ranges across cultures. In Palestine and in Finland, in Chechnya and in the US, in Palermo and in Milan. Naturally, we need to make distinctions. No matter how virulent, an Ultra site cannot be equated with the site of an armed Middle-Eastern group. Indeed there are great differences in terms of the language, diffusion, functioning and communicative effectiveness between the sites of extreme right, Middle-Eastern and Ultra groups (or, 'groups which have individualized war', as Ulrich Beck[17] has called them, providing a definition which has the double merit of being value neutral and of effectively capturing their modernity).

What I continue to be struck by is that although such websites have been present for some time on the Internet, they have received little attention from those who have a professional interest in studying communication via computer.[18] How come? This lack of research on such an important aspect of the Internet obviously cannot be attributed to distraction or to want of interest in recent developments in information technology and in the types of communication which flow along the network. The cause lies rather in the speed with which the Internet and, above all, the World Wide Web[19] are changing. And continue to do so, at an ever faster rate. With the result that

---

17 Beck, Ulrich (1992), *Risk Society: Towards a New Modernity* (London: Sage).

18 I can find no studies of Ultras' sites. On extreme right sites apart from the already mentioned essay by Enrica Cavina, see also Zickmund, S. (1997), 'Approaching the Radical Other: The Discursive Culture of Cyberhate', in S. Jones (ed.) (1997), *Virtual Culture* (London: Sage), pp. 185–205 and Tateo, L. (2005). 'The Italian extreme right on-line network: An exploratory study using an integrated social network analysis and content analysis approach', *Journal of Computer-Mediated Communication*, 10(2), article 10, http://jcmc.indiana.edu/vol10/issue2/tateo.html [accessed 25 June 2007 (translator)]. On Middle-Eastern combatants see two essays by Maura Conay: 'Reality Bytes: Cyberterrorism and Terrorist Use of the Internet', *First Monday*, available at http://www.firstmonday.org/issues/issue7_11/conway/, and 'Cybercortical Warfare: The Case of Hizbollah.org', available at http://www.essex.ac.uk/ECPR/events/jointsessions/paperarchive/edinburgh/ws20/Conway.pdf [both accessed 25 June 2007 (translator)]. On these sites see also, for information of a very different kind, the United States Institute of Peace Special Reports available at http://www.usip.org/pubs/reports.html [accessed 25 June 2007 (translator)] and the Institute for Security Technology Studies of Dartmouth College report 'Examining the Cyber Capabilities of Islamic Terrorist Groups' available at http://www.ists.dartmouth.edu/TAG/cyber-capabilities-terrorist.htm [accessed 25 June 2007 (translator)].

19 It is worth pointing out that the World Wide Web and the Internet are not the same thing. The Internet refers to a collection of computer networks of various kinds which are linked together, each of which has its own purposes. The World Wide Web, on the other hand, is a subnet of the Internet based on a graphical interface and the criteria of hypertextuality.

it can be said with certainty that there are many more things on the Internet and the World Wide Web than scientific research is capable of cataloguing or analysing. It is like working with a bacteria colony that is reproducing itself very rapidly in ways which are various and sometimes unpredictable. Thus rather than talking of the backwardness of scientific research in tackling this phenomenon we should recognize that this situation stems from the choice to privilege certain developments in the world of the Internet at the cost of others and that what will be learnt in this way will in any case prove useful for the exploration of territories which have been relatively neglected, like those which I intend to analyse in this book.

2. Once upon a time there was cyberspace

The most evident and important result of this research has been the jettisoning of the idea, for once and for all, of the Internet as cyberspace. An idea that afflicted the literature on computer-mediated communication for over a decade during which the only things that seemed to be online on the Internet – in the sense of being the object of study and discussion – were MUDs, chatrooms and newsgroups, that is to say, 'artificial' digital environments created by anonymous users all over the globe in order to interact with each other using only a computer and their imagination. Let me remind you briefly what these environments are. MUDs are game scenarios in which users can adopt fictitious identities and participate in complex adventures based on rules and instructions predefined by the inventors of the game; every move or action of the participants is the product of entering commands via a keyboard which can be read immediately by all the other players present at that moment in the MUD. Put more simply, MUDs were an electronic adaptation of board games, more specifically of those wargames invented in the '50s to simulate, with a wealth of detail, famous battles like Gettysburg or Waterloo. Chatrooms, on the other hand, are digital environments within which the participants can communicate directly between themselves in real time on some subject of their choice, again by entering texts via their keyboard. However, unlike MUDS, chatrooms do not involve creating, or collaborating in the creation of, some fantasy world, but involve simply entering into an exchange of messages with whoever is prepared to 'listen' and 'answer'. Newsgroups, finally, are electronic bulletin boards organized by theme which can be accessed by enrolled members when they choose in order to read messages posted by other members or to post their own, and

---

Webpages, which appear when you use a browser like Explorer or Mozilla Firefox, are the visual product of the combination of these two elements.

thus contribute to the particular collective discussion which distinguishes the given newsgroup.

These digital environments were certainly widely diffused on the Internet and indeed still continue to be so. But many researchers concerned with the Internet made the mistake of taking the part for the whole: they made generalizations concerning the web on the assumption that these environments were characteristic of the web in its entirety. The net thus became an ethereal location – usually called 'cyberspace' but sometimes even 'noosphere'[20] – populated by strange figures doing bizarre things. By men and women who chose to live in cyberspace day and night, changing their skins and identifying, merging, with the characters represented on the various digital stages, in a whirl of faces and masks which made them lose all contact with real life.[21] Or, in its most extreme formulations, by mutant subjects called 'cyborgs', cybernetic organisms, digital minotaurs, half men, half artificial, born of an anthropological mutation produced by the new information technologies. It was as if the Internet were able to produce real morphogenetic changes thanks to 'rhizomatic' processes of contamination between technological innovations and neurochemical states. In truth, I must admit that at the time these metaphors had a certain seductive power. Indeed, it was difficult to escape from thinking in those terms. A short time online was sufficient to make you feel as though you were being sucked into another dimension that seemed and often was really perceived as 'other'. I speak from personal experience as I can prove by telling you what happened to me one night many years ago. I remember that night as 'my journey with Fox in cyberspace'. I'll tell you about it in a minute. First a bit of background.

I talked one day with a friend about computers and the Internet and he referred to a programme called ICQ. ICQ is an instant messaging programme that enables two users connected online to exchange messages in real time. I had never used the Internet to 'talk' to somebody and I was curious about it. So I installed it on my computer and poked around in the menus until I discovered a function called Random Chat. It was a captivating discovery. It was sufficient to click on a series of buttons to make the name of somebody appear on the screen, sometimes accompanied by a brief description and a phrase that indicated his/her interests. After which, if that nickname or phrase stimulated your curiosity, you sent a message in which you asked

---

20 The term 'noosphere', was taken from the work of Teilhard de Chardin who, writing half a century before the Internet had an amazing intuition about the future of computers which were just appearing at the time. By noosphere he meant an integrated complex of technology, codes and systems of communication that would cover the whole world like an immense system of artificial thought. cf. Teilhard de Chardin's *The Future of Man* (1964), Image 2004.

21 cf. Turkle, S. (1995), *Life and the Screen: Identity in the Internet*, Simon and Schuster, and Markham, A. (1998), *Life Online* (Altamira Press).

whether they wanted to have a chat. In this way I 'talked' with people that it would normally have been difficult for me to have anything to do with. I chatted with American dentists and Pakistani engineers, with Malaysian programmers and German brokers. Until one day I had the idea of writing something in my presentation profile. Almost everyone does. Few people left the field beneath their nickname blank. I thought for a bit and then wrote: good advice free of charge. That's how I met Fox. One day, while on line, ICQ signalled the arrival of a message. It said something like: what would this good advice be? I answered, to what was still merely a number in an ICQ window, that first he would have to ask something and that only at that point would he discover how lucky he had been in meeting someone like me on the Net. In other words we exchanged wisecracks and the reciprocal authorization to insert nicknames in our list of friends. At that time I had – like most people – a 56k modem and I only went on line occasionally. But every time I connected, morning, afternoon or evening, ICQ signalled that Fox was online. And every so often I sent him a message and he replied. Things went on that way for a couple of months. I didn't know who he was. He wasn't curious about who I was. And then Fox began to ask me strange questions about artistic gymnastics. Did I like it? Or didn't I? Did I watch it on television? Frankly artistic gymnastics holds no interest whatsoever for me and as gently as I could I tried to make him understand that. But he persisted with artistic gymnastics. Then he went on to the gymnasts. And then finally to Romanian gymnasts. As anyone who has been unfortunate enough to watch an artistic gymnastics competition will know, gymnasts, and Romanian gymnasts in particular, resemble androgynous gnomes. Girls of 12 or 13 who have been subjected to all sorts of tortures from earliest childhood in order to enable them to do things which are totally unnatural on the beam or hanging from rings. I began to suspect that Fox was a shady character who was turned on by deformed young girls. I was wondering about this when ICQ opened a window and announced the arrival of a file. A JPEG file.[22] Fox had sent me a porno image, something really extreme, I was sure of it. I decided to risk it anyway and clicked on the download button. A few moments later the photograph of a girl who was evidently a gymnast – given her costume – appeared on the screen of my computer – a girl who was by no means unattractive. Love at first byte? Cupid had used the cursor? The arcane had revealed itself and shown a face that was far from being dark and disturbing. Fox had fallen in love with a Romanian girl during a visit to Romania and now spent all his free time chatting with her and writing her passionate emails as long as a Baricco novel. Hit by this media bombardment, the girl – but this is only my supposition – had to decide: is it

---

22 A file with the extension .jpg is a digitalized image. A file with the name cat.jpg is probably a photograph of a cat.

better to live in Romania teaching gymnastics or in New York as the wife of a computer freak? So Fox found himself on the horns of a dilemma: marry me or bye bye. And Fox didn't know what to do. And that's why he asked me for some 'good advice, free of charge'. And so I found myself in an embarrassing situation. To sum up: here was somebody I knew nothing about except that, according to what he had told me, he lived in New York and had fallen in love with a Romanian gymnast while visiting Romania. The love between the two which until now had found its nest on the Net consisted only in words written on the screen of a computer. But now it asked to return to earth and it manifested itself in the form of a pressing demand for marriage. And Fox didn't know what to choose. And asked me what to do, given that I claimed to supply 'good advice, free of charge'. I plucked up courage and threw myself into the business, leaving him, however, to draw his own conclusions. After a few days the Romanian gymnast had disappeared from our conversations. In compensation our chats became more frequent. Fox, I discovered, was a real cowboy of the keyboard, as William Gibson[23] puts it, able to get me to make a trip in a hot-air balloon in a MUD.

The idea of going up in a balloon came to Fox not only because he had read Julian Dibbell's book[24] about the experience, but also because he was an assiduous habitué of LambdaMOO, the most famous MUD in the world. He didn't know it very well – in any case it is impossible to know exactly all that there is in that MUD. But the idea appealed to him and he proposed it one evening via ICQ. So it was that we entered LambdaMOO and began to search. We separated. He went in one direction and I went in another. We kept in contact with each other partly using ICQ and partly using a communication command internal to the MUD. It immediately turned out to be an experience verging on the incredible. It only took a few minutes for me to feel sucked inside the screen of my computer. Nothing else existed. Only word messages between him and me and the experience of roaming through a forest of ASCII[25] images which catapulted us from one place to another. I was lucky. I was in fact the one who found the balloon. When I saw it I informed Fox who arrived a moment later. We got on board and off we went. For a marvelous journey in a country made only of letters, numbers and punctuation marks. You might believe that it takes a lot of imagination to

---

23 Gibson, William (1984), *Neuromancer* (New York: Ace Books).

24 Dibbell, Julian (1999), *My Tiny Life* (London: Fourth Estate).

25 An ASCII image is a picture created using nothing but ASCII characters – the standard character set for computers. Like this picture of Snoopy:

```
.--.__
| ;'__P
'.;(
| .)
';.L
```

think that you are really making a trip in a balloon in a programme like that. At the end of the day everything was drawn in ASCII. But many MUDs are full of images of this kind. And if you let yourself get involved in the game, if – like Alice – you pass through the looking-glass, then everything becomes believable. Even sailing across a sky and being able to look below and see the landscape beneath. For example, I suffer from vertigo and when I entered the command 'look down'[26] I felt a slight uneasiness in my stomach even though all that I could see was the very rudimentary two dimensional plan offered by the MUD. And, still stranger, I had to agree with Julian Dibbell's observation that the sky in LambdaMOO was an empty sky. In actual fact, when I entered the command 'look up', the MUD database replied 'There's nothing to see'. Yes, because no one had bothered to put clouds or birds or perhaps a slight breeze in that imaginary sky. Evidently the inhabitants of LambdaMOO, even if virtual, preferred to keep their feet on the earth rather that spending their time stargazing. A star. It was strange how navigating in nothing gave me a double sensation: that of amusing myself with a kid's game and that of having become suddenly omnipotent. But that was, and perhaps still is, the mystery and the attraction of these purely imaginary places. And at that moment I felt like a god. A god who could create things. Things that were real, like that balloon in which we had hung above LambdaMOO and which had been made by who knows who. So I decided to make a star and put it in that sky. I told Fox and he replied that it would be better if I made it on the ground. So I gave the command 'go down'. Let me state that then, as now, I am a dilettante in all things concerning commands, codes, languages, scripts etc. But like all dilettantes I was presumptuous and thought that it would be easy to do what I wanted. So, once I had landed – let's say – with my feet once again on the earth, I set to work at creating a star that would remain as a sign of my having visited that imaginary place. I had taken a quick look at the online help and I thought that I had understood everything. I typed in something like 'Create a star' and the database courteously responded, to my great satisfaction, that I had created object #3268 with the name star. Good, I chortled to myself, I've done it. It hadn't been difficult. I looked at Fox. He hadn't so much as batted an eyelid. I had hoped for a handshake and his congratulations. But he did nothing. I entered the command 'Look'. The database replied: 'You [description of the place where we were]. Fox is here'. And the star? Where had my creation gone? I entered the command 'Look' again but got the same reply. It could be that Pavel Curtis, the talented creator of LambdaMOO, had already arranged that if someone created a star or a cloud this would be automatically placed in the sky. I got back on board the ASCII balloon and went back up to check. There was nothing to

---

26 For the sake of clarity and to make things easier for the reader, the commands have been simplified.

see. I came back down. By now it was a question of principle. I had to find my star without Fox's help. I entered the command 'Examine #3268' and the database replied: 'Object #3268 is a star'. So it had to be somewhere. But where? I would even have looked in my trousers if I could have. But it wasn't possible. You don't have trousers or a jacket in a MUD. You are made of a substance that is volatile, of bytes, and you are represented by letters, numbers, and punctuation marks. A star cannot accidentally end up in your pocket (even if it could fit). I gave up. I asked Fox for help. Where had my star ended up? I asked him. He told me to enter the command 'Examined'. I did so. And the database responded with: '#3260 [that would be me], place [description of the place where we were], #3268 [the star]'. It was on me, that's where it was. Attached to Mr. #3260, that is to say, me. When you create something in a MUD, Fox explained, it is like making something with your own hands. And indeed it is like that. So if you look around, you see your surroundings but not yourself or what you are carrying. You want to see your star. Simply put it down. I did so. And now – Fox went on – go ahead and enter the command 'Look'. And this time my star was there, at my feet. Now let's go – said Fox – I want to take you on a trip to Brazil. What do you think? I agreed. I was about to enter the command 'Disconnect' but I stopped. I entered the command 'Look' again. The star was there. Shining. I entered the command 'Take the star' and only then did I disconnect from the LambdaMOO.

We left LambdaMOO behind us and flew to Brazil. We kept in contact by means of ICQ and email so that we could talk to each other. The idea of visiting a Brazilian chatroom was not, I admit, uncongenial. I had been using chat programs for sometime and I knew something about them. It had been my next step after ICQ. I had heard about chatrooms and I had been curious. So I had downloaded a program for the purpose and installed it on my computer. I remember very well when I first used it. After having clicked some buttons almost at random, I had seen the screen of the computer change its appearance and become white. And after a few seconds on that white page lines of text began to flow. And now I was embarking on the discovery of new territories. In Brazil. We arrived in – I believe – two or three nanoseconds. In those days there was a server called Rede Brasil. By connecting to that server the whole of the Brazilian network lay open before your keyboard. It was possible to visit Brazil, Brasilia, Recife and who knows how many other locations. I decided to enter the most obvious: Brasilia. I told Fox via ICQ but he didn't reply. I went through the necessary preliminaries on the main page and set about trying to find someone to talk to. There is, however, something that you have to take into consideration when using programs which communicate via computer in synchronous mode (that is to say in real time with people connected to the net in the same moment as you), namely, time differences. If you connect to a Brazilian chat room at ten o'clock in the evening Italian time, you have to remember that in Brazil it is five o'clock in the evening and that you will only find a certain sort of person. Once I connected at nine o'clock in the evening with an Australian chatroom. There it was nine in the morning of the following day and there weren't many people about, and those who were available were talking about their breakfasts. However, things were promising this time all the same. The main window was more or less the same as many others I had seen, but I was immediately struck by two things. The first was the number of colours that had been used. It really was a multi-coloured chatroom. Many of the texts were in colour and they had gone to town on ASCII art in colour. The second thing that struck me was the length of the nicknames. Our nicknames can't be longer than eight letters. There, in contrast, nicknames seemed to be of unlimited length. There were some which described by chapter and verse one or more aspects of the person – like: I'm tall, dark and I like pistachio ice cream – and others which described a personal desire: I've got a university exam tomorrow and I hope it goes well. However, I didn't manage to find anyone with whom to have a chat, an indication that they were all totally absorbed in private conversations. I was comforting myself with the thought that perhaps this was due to the fact that they didn't speak English when a window suddenly opened: tuberosa. Someone had read my greetings in English and now wanted to get to know me. Imagining that it could be anyone, I kept my distance and began with some formal pleasantries. Then tuberosa became bolder. Was I engaged or married? Ah! How much she wanted to come to Italy and meet fiery Italian stallions. Was I an Italian stallion? Things were certainly getting hot. Climaxing in: did I want to see her photograph to get an idea of her? Why, of course! I thought to myself. An image instantly appeared. Of Bugs Bunny dressed in a pink outfit with a bow between his long rabbit ears. 'Do you like me?' asked Fox. I began bombarding him with insults via ICQ and email. He replied via ICQ and email with messages which were filled with grinning little faces. Then he proposed going somewhere else. We went. I followed his track of bits in cyberspace: it was like following the tail of a comet in a starry sky.

That night was truly unique and incredible. We entered a Portuguese MUD, a Russian chatroom and then a Japanese one; we used ICQ to search for people and talked to four or five. I kept opening programs and windows. And at a certain point I felt a sense of vertigo. I didn't know who I was talking to any longer, where I was, who I was. I typed away furiously on the keys trying to answer this person or that, or to give a command, open my email, disconnect me, connect me, configure a programme. Some call it 'multi-tasking' but to me it seemed that I had really been sucked into what William Gibson calls a 'shared hallucination'. Fox, on the other hand, moved

about that space, that nowhere, with the lightness of a butterfly. He was
everywhere, but always master of the situation. Lucid. Calm. Technically
precise. Likeable to whoever he happened to talk to, in whatever situation he
met them. How did he do it? I was in a state of total confusion while he was
simultaneously discussing the international political situation with a Malayan
waiter in a South African newsgroup, chatting with a Russian hacker in a
Swiss forum, exchanging false photos of himself and his family via ICQ with
a Peruvian elementary school teacher, helpfully explaining how to decorate
a room in a New Zealand MUD, listing commands with precision and even
giving me some good advice on the colour of the sofa. In the end, that is to
say at nearly five in the morning, I was worn out. I sent a last message to Fox
to tell him that I was disconnecting and going to bed and he, seraphic, replied
that he was going to stay online for a bit longer. He was in the middle of a
discussion on NASDAQ trends in a Slovenian chatroom, and he was also in
the middle of a discussion with an interesting chap in an Odessa newsgroup,
so he didn't feel like ditching everything now. I understood. When I gave the
'disconnect' command I felt a little guilty. But if I had wanted to be polite,
and say goodbye to everyone I had been in contact with, it would have taken
me more than another hour and I wasn't capable of it. Not only was I half
asleep but I couldn't even remember who were behind those ten or twenty
windows that I had open. Real people? Ghosts? Words? A database? The
binary system multiplied by ten or twenty? When I finally had only a black
screen in front of me I felt a sense of relief. But it was only for a moment.
Already my right hand was uncertain whether to turn on the computer and
begin again. I was evidently running the risk of becoming a native, as an
anthropologist would say.

To sum up. In one night in Fox's company I wandered far and wide in
what was then called cyberspace. In fact, 1) we started from LambdaMOO,
2) then went to a Brazilian chatroom; 3) following that we moved on to a
Portuguese MUD, 4) a Russian chatroom and 5) a Japanese one; then Fox
moved on to 6) a South African newsgroup and 7) a Swiss forum, while I
spent time 8) in a New Zealand MUD; and finally, while I disconnected, Fox
remained to chat 9) in a Slovenian chatroom and an Odessa newsgroup –
but 10) I don't want to exclude a quick visit to a Riyadh chatroom. I would
also add, on the basis of what I have seen reading scientific literature on
the period, that I was not the only one to have online experiences of this
kind. On the contrary, at that time experiences of this kind were by no
means rare. But such journeys were only made by a certain type of net user.
By the most curious and the most technologically savvy and, a detail that
should not be undervalued, above all by American users. That is to say, by
people who could draw on an older culture of information technology and
of virtual digital worlds than the European one and who were more used to

seeing the Internet as an instrument for widening the scope of their social relations. Particularly since, as many case studies have documented,[27] this was precisely the objective that many had in mind when they connected up to the net: that of opening a window onto a world of relationships which would otherwise have been precluded by the limits of everyday routine. That this should also turn into a game of identities in which everyone was free to choose the mask with which to present themselves on the digital stages of the Internet is another matter. The primary purpose still remained that of creating and keeping alive, for a certain time period at least, personal friendships, stable social relations, and sometimes even communities, on the net, based on shared interests with people scattered all over the globe. All of this having recourse to nothing more than a computer, a little imagination, written texts and the capacity of digital codes to represent, mediate and mix important aspects of life online with real life. In this way significant experiences could be had even if in an imaginary context mediated by computer. Are there experiences which are not real? Or better, that are not perceived as real? In those days the reality of the online experience was never questioned. On the contrary, it was assumed that life on the net was as real as the everyday variety. That it was real life and not a deceitful simulation of it. Certainly, recourse was had, in the course of that explorative journey, to various strategies which made communication easier and more entertaining. Often, on connecting to the net, real identities were put in cold storage in order to assume others which appealed to you at that moment. For some, having recourse to an identity different from your usual one was synonymous with deceit, but early studies of computer based communication revealed, on the basis of empirical investigation, that this process by which people constructed their own identities was encouraged by the fact that the digital environments made available by the Internet were essentially playgrounds which permitted people to experiment with new forms of interaction and with new ways of presenting themselves. Playgrounds inside which it was possible to shelve for a few hours the social norms which regulate everyday life and at the same time to replace them with rituals of behaviour based both on a more or less conscious loosening of emotional self-censorship and of self-imposed normative limitations, and on a transfiguration of personal and social identity itself. In other words, according to those authors, you did

---

27 For example Baym, N. (1998), 'The Emergence of Online Community' in Jones, S. (ed.), *Cybersociety 2:0. Revisiting Computer Mediated Communication and Community* (London: Sage); Correl, S. (1995), 'The Ethnography of an Electronic Bar. The Lesbian Café', in *Journal of Contemporary Ethnography*, 3; Danet, B. (1998), 'Hmmm... Where's That Smoke Coming From? Writing, Play and Performance on Internet Relay Chat', in Sudweeks, F., McLaughlinge, M., Rafaeli, S. (eds), *Network and Netplay. Virtual Groups on the Internet* (Cambridge Mass.: The MIT Press); Clark, L.S., 'Dating on the Net', in Jones, S. (ed.), *Cybersociety 2.0. Revisiting Computer Mediated Communication and Community*, op. cit.

not present yourself on public stages in digital environments exhibiting your true physical, personal and moral qualities; you did not interact with other people online on the basis of the same codes of social conduct to which you were subject in real life. You presented yourself as someone else in a sort of consensual simulation, in which you amused yourself with challenging, manipulating, altering, dismantling and recomposing the principal pieces of your everyday dimension and the rules that governed it in order to construct a collective and imaginary dimension quite different from it.

On this subject, known as identity online, shelves and shelves of books have been written. Books that are undoubtedly useful for understanding the early use of the Internet as a means of communication, but as David Guantlett wrote back in 2000 'books continue to be published on how no one knows who we are in cyberspace, which is certainly something interesting even if also rather obvious. But how many books do we need saying this?'[28] And in fact this almost maniacal concentration on the topic of identity online and on the closely related topic of virtual communities, distracted many from recognizing what was maturing, almost in the same period of time, in other places on the Internet. Many users, encouraged by the fact that providers had begun not only to provide free connections to the Internet but also space on their servers and instruments for the purpose, were beginning to create personal websites. No more obscure commands to remember. No more austere black screens filled only with words. No more need to rack your imagination for ways of seeming attractive or interesting to strangers. Having a presence on the Internet, communicating through the net, was becoming easier, something within the reach of all. And indeed many did not let the opportunity escape them. Thanks to Tim Berners-Lee, the inventor of the World Wide Web, it was now possible to address not only a 'someone', perhaps a person or a group of people encountered in some limited digital environment, but the whole world, or at least that undifferentiated multitude that possessed a computer and a connection to the Internet. And so it was that there was a great flowering of multi-coloured webpages, a veritable flood of pages full of photos of exotic vacations, images of wives, children and cats, descriptions of musical or literary tastes, lists of hobbies, unpublished poetry and short essays of every kind. All of it framed with attractive graphics and rich in clickable references – called links – to other webpages. The destiny of these pages, however, was a foregone conclusion. Carried along on the unstoppable rising tide of WWW which grew exponentially every day, they were difficult to find in the portals like Tripod or Geocities which hosted them. They were like unknown islands – except to friends and relatives – which those who navigated on the web would only discover by chance. But

---

28 Guantlett, D. (2000) (ed.), *Web Studies: Rewiring Media Studies For the Digital Age* (London: Arnold), p. 6.

what did it matter? You could always hope to get lucky like Mahir Cagri who suddenly became, without wishing it, a star of the net.

3. Mahir Cagri's webpage

The story of Mahir Cagri is a curious one and merits being told. Mahir Cagri – of uncertain age and profession, although some say that he is an accordion player, weight 78kg, height 1.84 metres, green eyes, resident at Izmir, the most highly populated city in Turkey, telephone number 905352930004, email mahir00@yahoo.com – one day in 1999 (not specified) decided to create his own webpage.[29] There's no doubt about it: it was an unquestionably ugly webpage. For a background Mahir used a wall of bluish bricks. Right in the centre, dominating the page, was a full figure shot of him which portrayed him in a rather rigid pose despite the smile that escaped from under his bushy moustache. He wore black trousers, a double breasted brown jacket, a shirt that was presumably scarlet, and a black tie with yellow stripes. A blue silk handkerchief stuck out of the jacket pocket. The text under the photograph states in decidedly broken English: 'I like music, I have many many music enstrumans my home I can play. I like sport, swiming, basketball, tenis, volayball, walk'. Mahir's real stroke of genius, even if he didn't know it, lay in what he wrote above the photo as a heading for his webpage:

> This is my page…….
> WELCOME TO MY HOME PAGE !!!!!!!!!
> I KISS YOU !!!!!

For some unfathomable reason the phrase 'I Kiss You' and all those exclamation marks became in a short time a magnet that attracted visitors from every corner of the globe. In its peak week, soon after its appearance, Mahir Cagri's webpage registered 285,000 visits, an incredible number almost on a par with those of an ordinary search engine at that time. In other words, Mahir Cagri had constructed a webpage which enjoyed a success that was as extraordinary as it was unexpected, and which was accessed by swarms of navigators every hour of the day and night. Perhaps surprised himself by such sudden popularity, Mahir thought that his fans deserved something better to see and after some months he decided to make some improvements to his website. The restyling didn't amount to much, however. It was limited to the removal of the bluish brick background and its replacement by a more sober white background, and the addition, on either side of his photo, of a greenish icon with Turkish script. Everything else remained unchanged.

---

29 The page is still available at http://www.istanbul.tc/mahir/mahir/ [accessed 25 June 2007 (translator)].

You don't change a winning formula, he must have thought. If so, he was certainly right. The success of his site was not only consolidated, it grew, as the setting up of numerous mirror sites[30] here and there on the Internet testified. And as was also shown by the subsequent appearance of many imitations of his homepage. There were those who did no more than copy it slavishly, substituting their own head for that of Mahir, thus producing a sort of primitive digital photomontage;[31] there were those who used it as a model for a more personalized version;[32] and finally there were those who produced variations on the theme in ways which were sometimes amusing and sometimes not.[33] But the story didn't end there. On the contrary. Riding on the crest of a notoriety of planetary proportions that brought Mahir Cagri an entry in the Guinness Book of World Records for having registered 12 million visits to his site, there appeared (in the order of their birth): online games,[34] a Mahir Web Ring[35] with 54 active sites in 2002 and a Mahir Fan Club.[36] Seven years have passed since then and today Mahir Cagri is apparently a happy man, at least judging by his appearance on his new webpage which is decidedly more professional.[37] Lying on the lawn of an English-style garden, in the act of taking off his sun glasses, wearing a polo shirt of an acceptable colour, he is a different person who now presents himself like this:

WELCOME TO RECORD BREAKING
WEB SITE OF MAHIR !!!!!!!!!!
Ma•hir (Maa-heer): 1. First internet celebrity of the world 2. King of blogging.

---

30 A mirror site is a website that faithfully reproduces another. Usually this is done when it is thought that a site might be closed for some reason. In other words, it is a survival strategy for keeping sites online which might otherwise disappear. In the case of Mahir Cagri, however, mirror sites were used to promote and spread the word about his site. For an example see http://www.jengajam.com/r/Mahir-Kisses-You or http://www.romlist.com/mahir/ [Both accessed 25 June 2007 (translator)].

31 See for example http://restlessmind.com/humor/mahir/mahirclaus/ [Accessed 25 June 2007 (translator)].

32 See for example, http://www.geocities.com/Hollywood/Film/3518/obimahirspoof. html, and http://jmourinho.no.sapo.pt [both accessed 25 June 2007 (translator)].

33 See for example http://thecheesemaster.tripod.com/mahir.html [Accessed 25 June 2007 (translator)].

34 See for example http://www.newgrounds.com/assassin/mahir/ [Accessed 25 June 2007 (translator)].

35 See for example http://b.webring.com/hub?ring=mahir [Accessed 25 June 2007 (translator)]. A web ring is a group of websites that each contains links to the next, in circular fashion, typically all dealing with the same subject.

36 See http://groups.yahoo.com/group/mahirsfanclub/ [Accessed 25 June 2007 (translator)].

37 See www.ikissyou.org/[Accessed 25 June 2007 (translator)].

I have summarized the story of Mahir Cagri because I find it emblematic – though exceptional – of what was emerging at the turn of the century concerning how individuals used the Internet. In fact, this story shows how the use of the World Wide Web as a means of communication capable of reaching every house in which there is a computer connected to the net has made it much more powerful than it was previously. With a minimal outlay on the necessary equipment and without need of a deep knowledge of information technology, anyone could become, like Mahir Cagri, a producer of communications and diffuse their own messages on a planetary scale. Whether these messages were read by someone on the other side of the world was another matter. The important thing was that now it was possible. Previously, you could search the net for information on different species of dinosaur, on the various editions of Pimandro by Ermete Trismegisto or on Miss World's vital statistics; you could send emails to your relatives and friends to find out how they were, or to your work colleagues to fix the date of the next meeting; you could buy innumerable types of merchandise and services – but now you could also become an author. Amateurish perhaps, but still an author of communications. To borrow a distinction made by Manuel Castells, one of the most acute observers of these changes, and of the social impact of the Internet, alongside the 'interacted', those who continued to patronize old media like television, radio and newspapers and the limited prepackaged choices they offered in terms of information and communication, a new 'interacting' generation had appeared, those who were able to exploit the potential of the net, on the one hand to select what they wanted, and on the other to construct their own communication circuits.[38]

Naturally the web was not populated solely by pages created by aspiring web authors, even though their numbers were estimated in terms of millions at the turn of century. Alongside them was a growing number of what can be called 'public' webpages in order to distinguish them from private and individual webpages à la Mahir Cagri. These were websites created by industries, organizations and public bodies in order to publicize or sell products and services of all kinds. No studies of any kind exist concerning this type of webpage. As far as I know, only one study offers an estimate of their growth between 1998 and 2002. According to this research, public websites more than doubled in number over the period, from one and half million in 1998 to about 3 million in 2002, by which time they accounted for a grand total of one and a half billion pages.[39] In the years which

---

38 cf. Castells, M. (1996), *The Rise of the Network Society* (Oxford: Blackwell), p. 371.

39 See the study Trends in the Evolution of the Public Web, D-Lib Magazine, April 2003, available at http://dlib.org/dlib/april03/lavoie/04lavoie.html [Accessed 25 June 2007 (translator)].

followed, again according to this study, the number of webpages on the web stabilized at around that figure, a sign that rather than new and significant entrants appearing, a process of consolidation was taking place, involving the improvement of existing websites in terms of range and quality. In the light of this trend, and putting the matter metaphorically, the Internet was changing from an agora into a suk. From a place of communication and discussion into one of exchange and commerce. And what interest could sites like that – like, for example, eBay or Amazon – hold for those studying communication? Almost none, if you exclude those who are interested in studying the iconography of graphical interfaces. It is true that some people did try to study personal webpages,[40] but no one tried to do the same with public webpages, which thus remained the exclusive reserve of web designers and experts in online marketing. Among them, one person in particular has to be mentioned: Jakob Nielsen, whose name is indissolubly associated with a magic word: 'usability',[41] or how to construct websites in a clear, coherent way, without too many fancy frills, so as to ensure that access is simple and effective and that they deliver what they promise. You do this, not that. Forms, navigation bars, links, titles, texts, images, logos, banners: these are the things which, according to Nielsen, should be the object of interest and study. To give you an idea, here, for example, is what he says in a chapter entitled 'Screen Real Estate':

> When you view MapQuest [a website, my note] you find that most of the space on the screen ends up being used for fripperies which make you lose your concentration and are unrelated to the content for which the user comes to the site. Only 20 per cent of the 480,000 precious pixels of an 800x600 screen are used for content which interests this user.[42]

---

40 cf. Cheung, C., 'A Home on the Web. Presentation of Self in Personal Home Page', in D. Gauntlett (ed.), *Web Studies: Rewiring Media Studies For the Digital Age*, op. cit; Chandler, D., 'Personal Home Pages and the Construction of Identities on the Web', available at http://www.aber.ac.uk/ [Accessed 25 June 2007 (translator)]; Chandler, D. and Roberts-Young, D., 'The Construction of Identity in the Personal Homepages of Adolescents', available at http://www.aber.ac.uk [Accessed 25 June 2007 (translator)]; Miller, H., 'The Presentation of Self in Electronic Life: Goffman on the Internet', available at http:// ess.ntu.ac.uk/miller/cyberpsych/goffman.htm [Accessed 25 June 2007 (translator)]; Miller, H., 'The Hypertext Home: Images and Metaphors of Home on World Wide Web Home Pages', paper presented at the Design History Society Home and Away Conference, Nottingham Trent University, 10–12 September 1999, available at http://ess.ntu.ac.uk/miller/cberpsych/homeweb.htm [Accessed 25 June 2007 (translator)]; and Roversi, A. (2002), 'Le Home Page personali' in *Rassegna Italiana di Sociologia*, 1, 2002.

41 Nielsen, Jakob (1999), *Designing Web Usability: The Practice of Simplicity* (New Riders Publishing).

42 Nielsen op. cit.

Nielsen has even gone so far as to write a handbook that amounts to a prescriptive grammar of usability for which he claims universal validity, regardless of the kind of website or the characteristics of the visitor who navigates through its pages. Above all, he claims that his rules are objective because they are based on precisely measurable data, such as how much space is devoted to useful information and how much to that which is frivolous and superfluous. On the basis of laboratory tests during which he observed the way a certain number of people navigated a website, Nielsen came up with two hundred and twenty-two rules for the creation of websites that are truly usable or 'user friendly'. No flash animations, no frames, no JavaScript, no GIF images. If you use them you produce bad websites. In short, a sort of Lombrosianism applied to the world of the WWW based on measurement and digital physiognomy.

4. The birth of blogs

While the construction of personal webpages went gradually out of fashion and the WWW came to be dominated by portals, search engines and the websites of organizations, public and private bodies and companies, a new form of telematic communication appeared which has become increasingly popular in recent years. Blogs. What are they? A blog is a graphical form of communication via computer which is autonomously managed and which allows its creator to publish news, information and stories of every kind online in real time. Essentially they permit you to put your ideas and anything you find interesting on the web in a way that is quick and easy. Rebecca Blood, one of the first people to carry out research on blogs, describes them in these terms:

> Some provide precise descriptions of links that have been carefully selected. Some contain lengthy comments on the news of the day, punctuated here and there by links. Others consist in an infinite number of outpourings on the part of the writer. When links are included they take you to other analogous personal sites. Some are political. Some intellectual. Still others are comic. Some concentrate on a specific subject. Some are eccentric. Most are not concerned with making money and all are passionately involved in subjects they deal with.

> Blogs. What they have in common is a format: a webpage in which new contributions are positioned at the top and which is frequently updated, sometimes even several times a day. On the side there is often a list of links to other similar sites.

Some sites consist solely of one blog; in other cases the blog may be part of a more wide ranging site. Something more than a list of links but less than a full-blown magazine, blogs are difficult to describe but easy to recognize.[43]

If I had to draw up a rough typology, I would say that blogs can be divided into three main sorts: pure blogs, notebook blogs and filter blogs. Pure blogs are like diaries in a reduced form. Their content is very often the everyday life of the author, or some aspect of it, and this content is punctuated by links which are always subordinate to the text. And even when the links direct the reader towards some piece of news or an article published elsewhere on the web, the associated text always creates the impression of a quick and spontaneous comment. Notebook blogs, on the other hand, are more personal, more focused on the world that surrounds the author. They differ from pure blogs in the greater length of the texts, and in having a more specific type of content. The personal descriptions they contain often take the form of a story that unfolds over time. These blogs are shorter than an essay but longer than a comment and the writing is more thought-out than that in pure blogs. Both, however, concentrate on the personal world of the blogger or on their reactions to the surrounding world. It is therefore difficult to draw a demarcation line between them, if not for the fact that notebook blogs usually only contain one long comment per day. If there is a difference, I think it lies in the intentions of the blogger. Notebook blogs are in fact very similar to online diaries and they differ from the paper version only in the fact that they are published in such a way that anyone can read them. Someone who writes an online dairy aims to record events, explore their own interior world and do things that those who write diaries have always done with a pen and paper. Pure blogs, in contrast, usually consist of short comments and there may be several of them a day. Pure blogs, in other words, tend to be more concerned with communication than with personal reflection. That leaves filter blogs. These blogs have one element in common: they are based on links. Whether their authors write at length or whether they don't write at all, their objective is to take their visitors on a journey through the news. Some of them aim at clarity, others at completeness, but all, even those which use links as a base for the promotion of some political or philosophical position, concentrate on the external world. Graphically not much different from pure or notebook blogs, they reveal the personality of the blogger through the way in which they link to what is outside them. Their purpose, in fact, is to provide the reader with a continuously updated source of the news that is

---

43 Blood, Rebecca (2002), *The Weblog Handbook* (Perseus Publishing).

available online, on a particular subject which the blogger believes to be of importance.[44]

Having a blog is just as fashionable today as having a webpage was five years ago, and is much easier to create. In Italy, for example, all you need to do is go to the Splinder website, register, and with a few mouse clicks, 'your thoughts are online', as the portal claims. All for free. It is only necessary to choose the graphic format you like best – there are hundreds to choose from – and you can begin posting messages immediately. According to Splinder, one hundred thousand Italians were already dedicating time to this activity at the start of 2005 and if nothing happens to interrupt the trend of the last three years, that figure should double by 2006. And Splinder is not the only platform that is offering this service. Many portals which specialize in offering free Internet access together with an email account are now jumping on the bandwagon and permitting their clients to start their own blog. But the technical ease – as I can testify from personal experience – is accompanied by considerable cerebral effort. Naturally you can begin a blog and write what you want, when you want. But this would be a solipsistic exercise, almost certainly doomed to run out of steam in a short time. If, on the other hand, you want to use this instrument to communicate messages in the hope that others will read them, then the business acquires a totally different shape. It is important not only to be able to write something interesting but also to be constant in keeping your blog up to date. You may be ever so brilliant, acute, witty, and intelligent and so on, but if you cannot keep up a certain rhythm, which does not have to be daily but should be recognizable, someone who visits your blog once or twice will not return a third time, for the simple reason that they do not have time to waste checking whether you have written something new. In short, having a blog costs time and effort.

Naturally even blogs have their stars. I could name many famous bloggers, including some of the most highly regarded American journalists. I prefer to mention only two. *Massaia*,[45] an Italian blog which enjoyed a certain notoriety until it was abandoned by its author, I imagine out of exhaustion, which was the diary of a housewife who narrated all the tiny episodes of

---

44 On blogs, apart from the book by Rebecca Blood mentioned above, see 'Weblogs: a history and perspective' by the same author available at http://www. rebeccablood.net/ essays/ weblog_history.html [Accessed 25 June 2007 (translator)], Barret, C.(1999), 'Anatomy of a Weblog', available at http://www.camworld.com/journal/rants/99/01/26.html [Accessed 25 June 2007 (translator)], Winer, 'What makes a weblog a weblog ?' available at http://logs. law.harvard.edu/whatMakesAWeblogAWeblog [Accessed 25 June 2007 (translator)]. Finally, a collection of essays is available at http://www.klastrup.dk/archive/2004_02_01_archive. html#107634409840894819 [Accessed 25 June 2007 (translator)].

45 The blog is still visible [Accessed 25 June 2007 (translator)] at http://massaia.splinder. com. The last message was posted on 26 September 2003.

her daily grind, and, above all, *Where is Raed?*,[46] a blog of a very different
kind as it is concerned with war. When *Where is Raed?* first appeared many
believed it to be a fake, artfully constructed for some unknown purpose.
Doubts about it were only dissipated when two English journalists managed
to meet its author, Salam Pax, and told the story of a young man who, while
television stations and newspapers the world over were spending millions
of dollars on trying to understand what was happening in Iraq before and
during the Second Gulf War, was able to supply the world with a fascinating
description of life in a nation at war, in real time, with only a computer and
an ordinary telephone line. In fact, at the time Salam Pax was a twenty-nine
year old Iraqi architect living with his parents and brothers in Baghdad. His
best friend was Raed, a young Palestinian from Jordan whom he had met
while he was a student doing a post-graduate course in Jordan. Given the
international political situation communication was difficult and so Salam
conceived of the idea of beginning a blog concerning the latest news from
Baghdad in the hope that his friend would read it. Hence the decision to call
it *Where is Raed?*

During the first months of its existence the messages on the blog concerned
banal things: a certain person had got married, the author had had flu, he had
done this or that. Salam looked around him. He tried to find other Iraqi blogs,
or at least blogs in Arabic, and he realized that some did exist. But all they did
was talk of the Qur'an and of Allah. None of them commented on the events
which were looming on the horizon for Iraq. 'There was nothing about what
was happening here', he told the English journalists who found him. And so
it was that he decided to begin describing the more salient aspects of Iraq life
under the regime of Saddam Hussein. A very risky decision to take given that
about two hundred thousand people had disappeared for crimes much less
serious than openly criticizing the dictatorship. But, like many Iraqis, Salam
was used to danger. Four of his relatives had already disappeared. The year
before, for no apparent motive, one of his closest friends had been killed by a
person or persons unknown while driving his car. Two other friends had been
arrested: one had been released, nothing was known about the other. Salam,
however, decided to press on regardless.

There are many things that are striking about Salam Pax's blog. The first is
the irreverence it always showed toward Saddam Hussein's regime – which
gave rise to the suspicion that in reality a CIA or Mossad agent lay behind
it. While foreign journalists racked their brains over declarations of fidelity
made by unknown Iraqis in the street in an endeavour to find some sign of
dissent, Salam always treated those who governed Iraq with open contempt.
The second thing that strikes you is that contrary to the stereotype according

---

46 The blog is still visible [Accessed 26 June 2007 (translator)] at http://dear_raed.
blogspot.com.

to which Iraqis are poor, illiterate members of an underdeveloped society, in short very different and far removed from us in every respect, Salam turns out to be a young cosmopolitan, open to other cultures, attentive to events in the farthest reaches of the Western world. One small, but significant example: in one of his messages a few days before the outbreak of the war, he describes how he paid a visit to a music shop in Baghdad and bought five CDs including two by Western groups: The Deftones and the Black Rebel Motorcycle Club 'have joined the Pax Radio CD racks'. But time is passing and the war comes closer and closer. In one message he writes:

helped my mother pack things today. We have not decided to leave Baghdad if "it" happens but just in case we absolutely have to. We are very efficient packers, me and my mom. The worst packers are the emotional ones. The (oh-let's-remember-when-I-bought-this-thing) packers, we just do it in cold blood, we have done this quite often, we are serial packers.

Then on 25 March, four days after the beginning of hostilities, accounts of the first days of the war began to appear. The tone of the messages is much changed. And this quotation appears:

the West won the world not by the superiority of its ideas or values or religion but rather by its superiority in applying organized violence. Westerners often forget this fact, non-Westerners never do (Samuel P. Huntington).

Salam Pax has been called 'the Anne Frank of the war in Iraq', and someone added, 'its Elvis too', clearly with reference to Elvis Presley, because of his irreverent, ironic style of testifying to the dramatic facts of his time. 'Raed, do you really intend to stay in Jordan and miss everything? Come here and let's get ourselves bombed together', is a message that appeared at one point. Six months after the Americans entered Baghdad he wrote, 'The Americans are not in control of the situation. Two months like this is too much. Three would be a disaster'. 'They're not only paranoid. They are really crazy', he wrote of the Mukhabarat, the much feared agents of the Iraqi Intelligence Service. To sum up, whether he let rip against the inertia of his fellow countrymen or the against the behaviour of American or English soldiers, Salam always demonstrated an attention to detail and an absence of prejudice which made his blog indispensable for understanding the events of the Second Gulf War.[47] And at the same time he showed once again how an apparently "poor" instrument of communication could be transformed, in the right hands, into a

---

47 Salam Pax's blog messages were collected and published in a book that has been translated into many languages. In Britain it appeared in 2003 with the title *Baghdad Blog*, published by Atlantic Books in association with *The Guardian* newspaper.

formidable source of information capable of competing and, perhaps in this case surpassing, traditional media like newspapers and television.

But let's return to Italy and to Splinder given that it was precisely on Splinder that I carried out a small research project in February 2004 in order to find out to what extent blogs were used by people and groups of the extreme right. My curiosity had been stimulated by a debate between Splinder bloggers some months previously whose subject had been the appearance of a blog edited by Rimini Forza Nuova. Forza Nuova is well known. It is 'a national popular movement for the reconstruction of the homeland' which was born of a rib of Movimento Sociale – Fiamma Tricolore. It was founded by two right-wing activists, Roberto Fiore and Massimo Morsello, in 1997 on returning to Italy after a long sojourn in England, to which they had fled following their suspected involvement in the bombing of Bologna station in 1980. A local branch – that of Rimini – had opened a blog on Splinder and there were those who raised strong objections to its existence. I followed the whole discussion that arose out of this and it made me want to find out how a new form of telematic communication – blogs – could be used by an extra-parliamentary political group. And, above all, how successfully it was being used. From this point of view, Splinder seemed to be a good test bench. Were there many extreme right blogs on this platform? And how did they use it? Two simple questions to which I attempted to give a rough and ready answer. At that time, according to Splinder's homepage, it hosted about 45,000 blogs. It was humanly impossible to sift through all of them. So I put my trust in Google and Tim Berners-Lee, or in other words, in links. In part by seeing what came out of Google on entering certain key words, and in part by using links, starting with the first blog – that of the Rimini Forza Nuova – a picture emerged that was more or less the following. On Splinder there were a total of sixteen blogs that could be categorized as extreme right. Blogs which were in fact quite different from each other. Some had long been inactive – at least judging from the date of the last posting. Others were similar to public notice boards – containing, more than anything else, information concerning group meetings and initiatives. Others I included on the list because they were linked to the blogs of 'fascist comrades', even though their character was not of a markedly political nature. Certainly, occasionally, here or there a post popped up that was a bit out of the ordinary. For example, this appeared on the Forza Nuova Rimini blog, clearly in favour of summary executions:

One delinquent less. Bologna 6 February. A man, perhaps Kosovan, who failed to stop when the Carabinieri signalled him to do so, was killed after a long chase. The man turned abruptly waving a metal object and one of the policemen, fearing that it was a pistol fired and killed him. The incident occurred while the police were keeping a stolen car under observation.

Or a post on another blog which contained a eulogy to 'Ettore Mutti, fascist party leader'. Or an open defence of Fascism on yet another blog. But all in all, nothing of great moment.

There was, however, another thing that I noticed that seemed strange to me. It was a small blog ring which centred on a blog called Il Branco ('The Pack'). The structure of this ring consisted in a homepage – called Il Branco – two pages with identical graphics called 'Femmina Alfa' ('Alpha female') and 'Maschio Alfa' ('Alpha Male') and a fourth page indicated in the links as 'Maschio Beta' ('Beta Male'), but which referred to what was apparently a musical blog. The purpose of this ring was no clearer to me even after I had carefully read the various messages. The only thing that I discovered was that all the blogs directed you to another blog – not present on Splinder – which functioned as a 'collector' for the others. Finally, there was a blog to which other extreme right blogs often linked but which turned out to be practically empty except for a counter indicating the number of visits. I believe, however, leaving aside possible suppositions and considerations concerning content, that it is possible to draw this conclusion: blogs, or rather those blogs, were not yet an effective instrument for political communication. Blogs are, by definition, an instrument for communication of a rapid and dynamic nature; political communication requires other qualities, in particular a sizeable dose of 'stability'. It makes no sense posting a political manifesto to a blog – just to give an example – given that after a few days this document will be sucked into that black hole, the archive, and no visible trace will be left of it. From this point of view, webpages, full of images and documents which are always visible and accessible, seemed to me then, and still seem to me today, more functional, even if they are hybridized by other forms of communication.[48]

When I published the results of my little study on my own blog, the comments I received were quite measured and reasonable. The authors of some of the blogs I referred to in the study pointed out that in our country liberty of expression is guaranteed, and most people who intervened were largely in agreement with them. To this argument, undoubtedly legitimate, I took it upon myself only to add a postil. The Internet, this was and is my point of view, is a strange place made up of machines, abstruse programming languages, incomprehensible communication protocols – and also of people. People who use this complex technological apparatus to communicate. Many – the majority – use it in a positive way (at least for them – sometimes what they have to say is useless and boring for those who read them). Others use it in a way that is decidedly negative. Paedophilia, pornography and so on. We all know this. Paedophilia sites are obviously hidden away, and are difficult to trace, but the police are efficient in dealing with them. Pornographic sites

---

48 See Miani, M. (2003), *La comunicazione politica in Internet* (Roma: Sossella Editore).

are easy to access – if a lover of that sort of thing is willing to pay a bit
of money. But what about the others? Aren't they a problem? The people
who run them are free to distribute their pearls of hate and violence in
complete tranquillity. Perhaps that's how it should be. It's true that freedom
of expression is guaranteed by the law but it is still important to bring these
things to light. At least in this way we really know what we talking about.
And that is always a good thing.

In the case above I was referring to extreme right websites. The sites
of armed Middle-Eastern groups were not yet at that time being mentioned
on the evening news or in the pages of the national newspapers. But they
would be shortly. And with their appearance the picture, in a certain sense,
was complete. Now it was clear that the Internet had become a complex
communication receptacle, full of messages, symbolic content and information
of every kind. And that every one of these communicative fragments was
presented in a different way, for different purposes, by different people,
from different places. In short, it was now evident that if the Internet was
everywhere, it was not everywhere in the same way, and that the World Wide
Web had followed the same evolutionary pattern, transforming itself from
a *network* – a technological apparatus – as big as the world, into a *web* – a
communicative text – as big as the world.[49] A web into which many weavers
worked their designs everyday. The result was a tapestry whose patterns
could change rapidly but whose weave, for all its variety, was governed by
objectives and processes of logic that were clearly discernible – with a little
patience and attention.

5. The Internet becomes immanent

While I was carrying out these first experiments in research I happened to
read an essay that Barry Wellman had written together with Bernie Hogan,
entitled *The Immanent Internet*.[50] If it was Manuel Castells who buried the
metaphor that likened the Internet to cyberspace, Wellman was certainly
the man who wrote its epitaph. His work on digital cities, in particular on
Netville, a district of Toronto cabled with optical-fibre, on the everyday use
of the Internet and on the changes that have taken place in the construction of
social networks consequent upon the diffusion of new digital technologies,
represents a real point of departure for understanding what are today, in
concrete terms, the most relevant aspects of the *Network Society*. Obviously

---

49 I appropriate the image provided by the Moroccan sociologist Fatema Mernissi (2004)
in her book *Karawan. Dal desert al Web* (Firenze: Giunti).

50 Wellman B. and Hogan B., *The Immanent Internet*, available at http://www.chass.
utoronto.ca/~wellman/publications/index.html [Accessed 26 June 2007 (translator)]. Many of
Wellman's essays are available at the same address.

I'm not going to go into these themes at this point: I limit myself to mentioning the thesis that Wellman emphasizes at every opportunity and with which I am in full agreement, namely that many of the technologies associated with the Internet, starting with computers, have by now become banal artifacts, means of connection which have become part of our everyday life on a par with telephones and fridges. We don't use these technologies, Wellman says, to transform ourselves into cybernauts or into microparticles in the noosphere, but more prosaically in order to send an email to our grandmother or our girlfriend, order shopping at the supermarket or see the replay of a sporting event. In other words, as the title of his essay makes clear, there is nothing transcendental about the Internet. But he also adds that what is marvellous is that we can do all these things where we want to because one of the characteristics of this means of communication is its ubiquity. Take cell phones, for example. This kind of telephone is not connected to a socket in a room like a house phone: it can be carried around with us tucked into a pocket in our clothes. And so we can call and be called from any part of the world. Or take computers, thanks to wireless technology,[51] we can send emails or update our blog while comfortably seated in a café, or while waiting for our flight in a waiting room or while travelling on a train. These things represent an important change in our capacity to communicate with others. Thanks to these technologies and these instruments, communication can in fact become simultaneous. We don't have to wait any longer. We don't have to wait until the people with whom we want to talk get home or get to work. The place in which you are at the moment when you feel the need to talk to them becomes irrelevant if we know that they possess a cell phone. Wherever they are, they are immediately contactable. In the same way, we don't have to search for an access point for our computer if we have a laptop with a simple wireless card. We only need to turn it on and we can return to weaving our web of communications when we most feel like it. In this case, too, waiting has ceased to be a problem that impedes communication. Ubiquity and immediacy, in other words, have become the two space time coordinates which determine the way in which many people today communicate with each other. All of this has an important consequence: an increase in the degree of connectivity that is theoretically available to each of us. A connectivity which is quite complex to tell the truth, since it permits us to activate forms of one-to-one communication, as happens when we use a cell phone or send an email to a friend or relative, or one-to-many as happens when we write something to our blog or webpage, and which can be personalized, so to speak, both in terms of initialization and of exit. We can in fact decide when

---

51 Wireless communication refers to any means of communication in which the sender transmits a message using radiation that travels through free space, rather than there being a fixed conducting path to the receiver. Cell phones are a familiar example.

we don't want to be disturbed by a certain person or organization and thus activate filters which block messages which arrive from that source. At the same time we can ask a certain person or organization to send us messages which interest us on our cell phone or our computer. And this is also true when we are the source of transmission, given that, keeping to the examples mentioned above, we can decide to block certain telephone numbers or make our blog or our webpage visible only to some people or groups. In short, a malleable technology is at our disposal which enables us to open or close the door of communication at will, on the basis of our mood, our interests, our style of life and our ways of thought.

Wellman's essay ends with an assertion:

> Journalists often ask us: "Is this a good thing or a bad thing?" Our answer is, "It is just a thing". It will have good and bad outcomes. However, while the internet is immanent, its effects are not technologically predetermined or sociologically predestined. They are evolving and their use can be shaped by human decisions.[52]

This is an assertion that made me think, given that, in its apparent obviousness it implies a number of problems for scientific research. In my case, reading it, I could not help thinking about the material I had accumulated in the course of my research and asking myself a question, whether banal or not I can't say. The question I asked myself was this: are those websites of hate that I have seen every day only a collateral, perhaps a secondary, perhaps a negligible, certainly an undesirable aspect of the Global Village glimpsed by McLuhan and finally realized, as affirmed by Barry Wellman, with all the necessary reservations, or are they on the contrary a phenomenon that cannot be contained within this model? Couldn't they in fact be a glaring sign – though largely unnoticed – of the fact that with all the new technology which we have today at our disposal we haven't ended up creating a global village? That on the contrary, we have facilitated the development of that process of Balkanization that many recent political and economic events seem to have provoked it different parts of the world? Many sociologists have already warned us about this. Putnam, for example, has been saying just this for some time.[53] Social cohesion 'goes down' he argues, referring to the United States. But if you look around you a little you realize that this is not a purely American phenomenon. You don't need much sociological imagination to recognize that social cohesion has 'gone down' a bit everywhere. If this is true, then even the websites which I intend to study in the following pages could represent an example, limited perhaps, but nevertheless significant.

---

52 Wellman, B. and Hogan, B., *The Immanent Internet*, op. cit., p. 12.

53 Putnam, Robert (2000), *Bowling alone: The collapse and revival of American Community* (New York: Simon & Schuster).

The diversity of languages which emerges in such an overwhelming way across them does not seem to be compatible with the notion of a plurality of personalized cultures which in the course of time, forced to live side by side, will either come together through the creation of a sort of pidgin culture or find a way of living together in mutual tolerance thanks to the development of respect for reciprocal differences. These sites could represent, instead, a genuine testimony to the fractures which run through important parts of our planet, at varying depths and sometimes in interrelated ways. To turn Wellman on his head, this would not be merely an undesirable, and in many ways horrible, effect of a changing equilibrium between the tendency for social cohesion to weaken among people living in ordinary everyday contexts and the tendency to replace the physical and relational proximity that comes from face to face interaction with the greater ease of interacting with someone – whether geographically near or far – that comes from increased connectivity. When Wellman says in a laconic fashion that social cohesion declines but linear connectivity increases, in reality he is asserting that the connectivity that the Internet puts at our disposal is nothing other than the development of social cohesion by other means. In my opinion this is a half truth. It could be true for the inhabitants of Netville or of Catalogna that he studied. And there is no reason to doubt it given the quantity of empirical evidence that he provides to support his case. But if we look elsewhere things appear in a different light. When, for example, after the civil war which dismembered Yugoslavia, I tracked for some time a number of newsgroups like soc. culture.bosna-herzgvna and soc.culture.croatia, what was it that struck me most forcibly on reading the posted messages? The glaringly obvious fact that the different electronic communities expressed a degree of intolerance and reciprocal contempt equal if not superior to that of their ethnic groups of origin. And it was through monitoring these newsgroups that I formed an image of the net – which by definition should be without barriers that divide and separate – as a place where, on the contrary, they can persist and where they continue to reflect the same historical divisions, the same geographical barriers and the same forms of incommunicability that exist in many regions in the world. In short, just as Yugoslavia has been Balkanized, in the same way, in my opinion, wide sectors of the net are being Balkanized too.[54]

Agreed, the examples upon which I base these assertions are extreme. But they exist and they are not negligible in number. And, what is more, they are successful, very successful. They are not volatile presences of which no

---

54 When I use the term Balkanization I mean the fragmentation of a given population into separate and structurally divided groups. In this case I am referring to a population which is very wide and of supranational dimensions. In using the term I owe a debt to M.Van Alstyne and E.Brynjolfsson who first used it in their essay 'Electronic Communities: Global Village or Cyberbalkans?' available at http://www.si.umich.edu/.

trace is found the second time you try to visit them. They are always there, at the same web address.[55] You can bookmark them and with a click they will reappear on your computer screen. They are visited by thousands or perhaps hundreds of thousands of people who do not come upon them by chance but who have deliberately looked for them because they identify with and find themselves mirrored in their content. It confirms yet again an old axiom of the sociology of communication: communicating is only in part about the transmission of messages or information to a certain number of people in order to increase their knowledge. And being informed only means in part knowing what happens in the surrounding world. For a long time it was believed that the significance of communicative acts was rather different: that it lay in distributing messages and information across greater or smaller distances so that people would know more. As is well known, this was an idea that went back to the time when the term 'means of communication' meant above all things like roads, bridges, trains and machines and that it only came to refer to the content of communication when the first print publications appeared. But today we know that things are not that simple. We know that being producers or recipients of communications also means participating in a ritual. And as a ritual it is associated with terms like 'sharing', 'participation', 'association' and 'possession of a common faith'. This way of seeing communication is rooted in the affinity of terms like 'communion', 'group', 'community' and defines it not so much or merely as an act involving the propagation of information, as an act involving participation in shared beliefs. That is to say, when we read a newspaper article or watch the evening news, we don't do this first and foremost to acquire information and become informed about things which are more or less important concerning our life or that of others. That element is undoubtedly present but it is secondary with respect to the principal objective which we have which is that of – to use the words of James Carey – 'participation in a mass'.[56] In other words, communication is an act through which we learn little that is new but thanks to which we can once again confirm our adherence to a certain point of view and to a particular system of values or to a particular ideology.

There, then, explained in terms that are still very general but which I will try to flesh out in the following chapters, is why, for example, one-time Kurdish shepherds are capable of constructing websites that Jakob Nielsen, I'm sure, would define as lacking in usability but which nevertheless have planetary impact. As we shall see, the information content of this kind of site, which I include for the sake of expositional economy under the common

---

55 With the exception of the websites of armed Middle-Eastern groups for a reason that I will explain in the fourth chapter but which should be easily guessed.

56 Carey, J.W. (1988), *Communication as Culture: Essays on Media and Society* (London: Routledge).

heading of 'hate sites', is usually quite low and in some cases almost nothing. Their efficacy lies rather in their capacity to bring to the surface and render once again operative the ancient distinction friend/enemy, us/them, who is with us/who is against us. They establish the boundaries of membership and the criteria which delimit them. In this way they force us to take a position. Whether they are concerned with faith in a football team, fascist or Nazi ideology or the political situation in the Middle East, these sites confront us with a choice which is both radical and exclusive. They do not permit an open rational debate of differing opinions that would open their positions to discussion. The content menu they offer their visitors, wide ranging though it may be, is not modifiable. They offer us only closed universes of values which are accepted or rejected en bloc. Which is not really a good example of democratic communication.

But the moment has now come to enter more directly into these issues. I will do so by making public what I have observed in the course of my journey through the hate sites. It was not a pleasant journey. I hope, however, that my account of that journey, which I offer here, will prove useful to my readers.

Chapter 2

Football Fans on the Net:
Ultra Websites

1. Wednesday 29 May 1985

I can pinpoint exactly when I began to concern myself with football violence and with Ultra groups. It was at nine o'clock on the evening of 29 May 1985. It was a Wednesday. What happened that evening, at that time? And where? I'll tell you in a moment. First I want to make a confession.

And it is this: for a long time I loved football. I often went to the stadium on a Sunday afternoon to see the team of my city play. And sometimes I also went to an away game. There were many things that I liked about football. First of all, what surrounds it. In spring I used to like going to the stadium early and being blinded by the green of the still empty football field. A crystalline green so green that it hypnotizes you. And on winter afternoons I enjoyed seeing the field wrapped in a misty luminescence. The pitch was for me a thing alive and vibrant. I used to like to watch the buzzing crowd entering the stadium and arranging themselves on the terraces. At first little blobs of colour scattered here and there around the rectangular pitch, slowly, slowly becoming a compact mass that formed a single body. Elias Canetti[1] has written that a football stadium is a place in which people come together in a ring and turn their backs on the city. It's true. For those magical ninety minutes I saw thousands of people who were no longer 'townies'. They had shed that role and had become members of a brotherhood united in the celebration of a unique and unrepeatable rite. The rite of the goddess *Eupalla*,[2] as the famous Italian football journalist Gianni Brera would have called it, whose sacred elements are fortune, agon, hubris and nemesis. There, in that place, all the things which make life unpredictable and ineludible are displayed before you in the shape of twenty-two men dressed in coloured strips kicking a leather ball. With this simple act they have the gift of dispensing joy, happiness, pain, excitement, anger and sadness. But I liked football also for another reason.

---

1   Canetti, E. (1963), *Crowds and Power* (Viking).

2   The Goddess of football, or rather of the beauty of the game (from the Greek 'eu' = good).

When you think about it, football is an unnatural game. This is an obvious observation. Feet serve to give movement to the body. Their function is that of permitting us to move horizontally or vertically at varying speeds. Given this limited functionality, our feet are equipped with a ridiculously small number of nerve cells compared to those which govern our joints or our ability to grasp things. This has an important consequence: it is difficult to control an object with an organ that is so disadvantaged. Yet it is precisely this ability, the use of feet to construct those actions which constitute the plot of the game, that is exhibited, with greater or lesser skill, every time two teams face each other on a football pitch, whether it be in a great stadium before thousands of spectators or on an anonymous football field in the periphery. It's something everyone knows. Almost all the athletic feats performed by football players consist in no more than hitting a leather sphere with their lower limbs, or very occasionally with their heads, and coordinating their movements with their trunks so as to give the ball the trajectory they want. However good they are one thing is obvious: football is not a natural game. On the contrary, it is a difficult, technical game. And, it may be added, it is precisely this aspect which confers upon it both the fascination of being unpredictable and the beauty it often manifests.[3] And the history of football is there to prove it, packed with episodes in which the little guy has taught the giant a lesson or a lanky, black man has silenced an opponent who seems to have been carved in Greece.

By now you will have cottoned on. I was a 'football fan'. I too belonged to that race of people who some look down upon with a mixture of scorn and arrogance, judging them clearly inferior. Fortunately for this despised category of person, the English writer Nick Hornby has shown that football fans are basically people who are absolutely normal.[4] Disturbing another English writer I could say, 'Hath not a football fan eyes? Hath not a football fan hands, organs, dimensions, senses, affections, passions? Fed with the same food, hurt with the same weapons, subject to the same diseases, healed by the same means, warmed and cooled by the same winter and summer as a Christian is? If you prick us, do we not bleed? If you tickle us, do we not laugh? If you poison us, do we not die?' Exactly. 'If you poison us, do we not die?' I would change the last line: 'And if we are attacked or stabbed or beaten with sticks, do we not die?' I would change it because on that Wednesday, on 29 May 1985 at nine in the evening local time, for the first time, like many other people the world over, I saw football fans die.

I well remember that evening. The day before I had gone to another city for a conference. On the 29th I got up early to go home. I got in the car

---

3   Perhaps I exaggerate, but I am convinced that Piola's famous scissor-kick would not be out of place in an art gallery.

4   Hornby, N. (1992), *Fever Pitch* (Gollancz).

and got onto the motorway. Suddenly I became aware that on the opposite carriageway, the one going north, a long procession of coaches was passing. There must have been about 15 of them. They were full of Juventus fans going some place. The coaches were decked out with flags and banners of every description. Many fans were hanging out of windows waving their black and white flags. Some shouted slogans that were lost in the noise of the traffic. I wondered where they were going. Then I remembered. That evening there was the final of the European Cup against Liverpool. In Belgium. In Brussels, to be precise. I am not a Juventus fan, indeed I am very far from being a Juventus fan. But a game between a strong Italian side and the Reds was a spectacle not to be missed: that of the 'red furies' attacking with deep crosses, a little imprecise but always dangerous, and the 'gobbi' with their black and white strips defending but capable of lightning counter-attacks, perhaps launched by Platini, a player who can put a ball at the feet of another player from a distance of forty metres. Naturally with the sound turned off and Mozart at low volume for background music. Why? For two good reasons. Firstly, because it is pointless to listen to commentary that tells fractionally after the event what you can see with your own eyes. Secondly, because, let's be truthful, Mozart wrote a lot of music to maintain his family and make a few coppers. Certainly a great composer but some of his works are not very demanding. So Mozart so as not to disturb my concentration but to create a bit of atmosphere all the same. The concerts with horn and orchestra. Repetitive music which when played at low volume doesn't intrude or disturb. (Some years ago a national television channel on a Sunday afternoon showed brief summaries of the games played that day without a commentary but only with the live audio of the spectators. It worked. It worked very well. Much better than the commentary and comments of some player in retirement.)

The last coachful of Juventus fans had by now disappeared from my rear mirror. I spent the afternoon doing various things and getting on for 20.00 I set off for home. I didn't hurry and so it was already 20.50 when I put my key in the lock, opened the door and put on the lights. I didn't have time to have the shower I had wanted all day. I quickly took off my work clothes and put on something comfortable. Five past nine. I thought that I had missed the beginning and I hurried to put on the television. A few seconds later, sharp and clear, images of Heysel Stadium in Brussels appeared on the screen. The game had not yet begun.

It is difficult to describe what I saw on the screen. In those days I didn't have a video recorder (had they been invented?) and I haven't been able to see a video recording of the tragedy. The only thing that I have is the transcript of the commentary on the game which was by Bruno Pizzul, and of his conversations with the studio in Rome where his interlocutor was Franco de Laurentis.[5] I can only summarize the events as I saw them happen on television. So to begin: on the evening of 29 May 1985 the European Cup final was to be played between Liverpool, an English club, and Juventus, an Italian club, at Brussels in the Heysel Stadium. Apart from a certain number of Belgians, the stadium contained a lot of supporters of both clubs. Already in the afternoon there had been clashes between the two groups of supporters but the situation did not seem serious. Skirmishes between opposing groups of supporters before a game were already quite common in those days and the Belgian police had managed to keep things under control. The serious or rather, dramatic, events happened inside the stadium and were principally due to a fatal error of judgment on the part of the organizers of the match. At first the fans entered the stadium normally and without incident. All that remained was to fill one sector behind the goal – section Z. Into this section – and this was the error which cost the lives of 39 fans (38 Italians and a Belgian) – supporters of both Juventus and Liverpool were made to come and thus found themselves side by side separated only by a thin cordon of Belgian police. But there was a detail that none of the organizers had taken into consideration. The Juventus fans were normal football fans: young people, old people, men, women, children. The Liverpool supporters beside them were apparently hooligans, young fans who were particularly violent and who behaved accordingly. And they too made a mistake. Thinking that they were faced by Italian Ultras they did what is done when two factions of young fans meet: they attacked. But – as I said – they did not have Juventus Ultras in front of them – they were in another section of the stadium – only simple, normal Juventus supporters. Who, when they saw first objects of all sorts raining down on them and then that they were being attacked by a multitude of drunken madmen carrying all kinds of weapons, lost their heads and panicked. And fled. Many ran towards the external perimeter of sector Z and massed against the little protective wall there, which, under the pressure of such numbers, collapsed. They were pitched below by people pushing against them. A rain of human beings smashed on to the pavement below. Others tried to escape, swarming against the fence that separated them from the pitch. This too gave way and anyone in front was crushed under the weight of the fence and of the people who poured over it in the hope of saving themselves by reaching the playing field. A scene that I remember well. A man, or better, the trunk of a man, sticking out from under the fence. On which a pile of people had formed. Imploring for help. For someone to help him to get out from under the fence because he was clearly immobilized. You could not hear his voice, but it was clear that he was terrified. Two or

---

5   See 'Lancillotto e Nausica. Critica e storia dello sport', **1**, 1986, p. 26, foll.

three people tried to pull him out by the arms but it was useless. He didn't budge an inch under the weight that pile of humans. There followed other scenes, all full of crushed bodies, bleeding, like lifeless puppets. As I have said the final toll was 39 dead and over 200 injured. All for a game of football which was not interrupted. It was only the beginning of a long trail of blood that was destined to stretch on in time.

2. The black curve[6]

I'm not going to launch into a history of football hooliganism at this point, or even of football hooliganism in Italy – which dates from the beginning of the '70s and has gone through various stages and forms. There are already many books on the subject.[7] I shall limit myself to mentioning two episodes which I think give an idea of how it has changed. First episode: 28 October 1979, Stadio Olimpico, Rome. The Roma-Lazio derby. During that game a 39-year-old Lazio fan, Vincenzo Paparelli, married with three children, died. He was killed by a flare fired from the opposite curva, that occupied by Roman fans, who had begun taking pot shots at the enemy curva. The first missiles fell short. Until Giovanni Fiorello, a 19-year-old Roma fan took over. He was definitely a better marksman. His flare flew in a perfect arc from one end of the ground to the other and ended its trajectory in Paparelli's left eye. He died a few minutes later. A crime had been committed. The first in a series that continued over the course of several years and cost nine lives. This macabre book-keeping does not take into account those who met their deaths for reasons which did not involve a direct confrontation between opposing fans. Like, for example, the young men burnt to death on a train taking Salernitana fans home after an away game in Piacenza in 1999. It had been set on fire, whether out of madness or idiocy, by some of the same Salernitana fans.

Second episode: again at the Stadio Olimpico in Rome. Again a Roma-Lazio derby. But now it's 28 March 2004. The game is interrupted by an invasion of the pitch on the part of three Roma fans who invite – to put it mildly – the players not to continue the derby because a child has been killed by a police vehicle. The news is false but in any case the match is suspended. Public opinion is shocked and disconcerted. The politicians are

---

6   The curva (pl. curve) are the terraces or stands with reduced ticket prices behind the goals in a football stadium. Loyalty to the curva (the stand in which the group is located, sometimes called kop in Britain) is fundamental to Ultra mentality.

7   To mention but a few: Dunning, E. et al. (2002), *Fighting Fans. Football Hooliganism as a World Phenomenon* (Dublin: University College Dublin Press); Brown, A. (ed.) (1998), *Fanatics! Power, Identity and Fandom in Football* (London: Routledge); Roversi, A. (1992), *Calcio, tifo e violenza. Il teppismo calcistico in Italia* (Bologna: Il Mulino); Dal Lago, A. (1990) *Descrizione di una battaglia. I rituali del calcio* (Bologna: Il Mulino).

indignant. The football world is outraged. The usual nonsense. But there was something that went unnoticed. Roma and Lazio fans are notorious for being bitter enemies, especially since Paparelli's death. That Sunday, however, peace reigned. It was too peaceful. When the news spread, the Lazio fans removed their banners from the stands, waited for the match to be suspended and left the stadium in silence. The Roma Ultras watched the pitch invasion by their companions and once the match had been suspended, left the ground as well. Outside, both groups indulged in the new Ultra sport of fighting the police. But there was something that did not quite add up in these events. Apparently. To make sense of it all, you need to know who the three Roma pitch invaders were. The names of two of them are known. Who were they? The first, apart from being a Roma Ultra, was a member of the extreme right group 'Tradizione e Distinzione' ('Tradition and Distinction'). The second was a member of another extreme right group called 'Opposta Fazione' ('Opposing Faction'). And they were two of the leaders of the Roma Ultras. At this point things are a bit clearer. There have always been extreme right groups among Lazio's fans. Well, let's name names: the 'Irriducibili' (the 'Diehards'). The Roma fans have become like them thanks to the infiltration of Forza Nuova elements. And now the two groups of fans are united in the struggle. And with that pitch invasion and the consequent suspension of the match they sent a message to all Italian Ultras: we are united, we support the extreme right and we are so strong that we can get a game suspended when we want to.

How can I assert that this is how things stand? I can do so because I have seen the webpages of the two groups. Let's begin with the Roma Ultras. They have a site that you can find at the address http://www.asromaultras. it/.[8] It seems like an ordinary Ultra site, rich in subsections: the history of A.S.Roma, championships and trophies, historic matches and so on. It is not lacking in photos of past and present footballers and news about the current season. But half hidden amongst this stuff there are a number of additions. The first is http://www.asromaultras.it/tradizionedistinzione.html. That's right: Tradizione e Distinzione. In appearance it's a page that is similar to that preceding it, but clearly visible, top centre, is a link: http://www. tradizionedistinzione.it. When you enter this site the first thing that appears is the figure of bare-chested, muscular man flanked by a series of images in sequence of fans and police, followed by a quote from Ezra Pound: 'If a man is not prepared to run risks for his ideas, his ideas come to nothing and he is worth nothing'. I won't describe the other features which distinguish this site. I'll limit myself to mentioning that in the section 'Recommended

---

8   Accessed by the translator 26 June 2007.

reading', Franco Freda,[9] that well-know lover of non-violence and promoter of democracy, occupies the place of honour at the top of the list. Still on the same Roma Ultras site there is another addition: http://www.asromaultras. it/oppostafazione.html, an 'Opposta Fazione' page. Their motto, carried by the site and printed on the scarves that they wear at the stadium, speaks for itself: 'Many enemies, much honour'.

I have mentioned these two Roma-Lazio derbies because they are emblematic of how the world of the Ultras has changed in the course of the years. If at one time it was a world which permitted friendships and forms of aggregation created elsewhere (in districts of the city, in bars, in associations, in youth centres) to be taken inside the stadium for remoulding according to the codes of behaviour of the terraces and experiences matured outside the stadium were reworked in terms of recurrent thematic models – by the choral absorption of the stadium, by the totalizing sense of being an Ultra, by the obsessive and – why not? – openly violent slogans, by a reassuringly Manichean vision of the world (us fans of [name of team] vs. everyone else), so as to continually repopulate the imagination of young Ultras with new mythical figures and new symbolic content based specifically on football, now things are very different. Radical right groups have always been present on the terraces but theirs was a presence circumscribed to some groups of fans (above all, of Inter and Lazio) which held little attraction for the wider Ultra movement, if for no other reason than because their political culture drew inspiration from the right-wing extremism of fascism and Nazism, a culture which had little to do with the symbolic universe of the Ultra movement or, more generally, with the political and social climate of Italy. Recently, however, as I have said, the situation has changed, and it has changed profoundly. For two reasons, I believe. In the first place, the face which extreme right groups now show on the terraces in Italian stadiums – and for that matter on terraces in other European countries – no longer has fascist or Nazi features. They now draw on a nationalism and a xenophobic racism that is shorn of any nostalgic ideology. Not by chance those responsible for the promotion and diffusion of this new form of extremism, much more in step with the spirit of the times, are to be found prevalently among the Ultras of north-east Italy (that is to say of the Ultra supporters of teams like Verona, Padova, Treviso, Pro Patria, Triestina or of the minor teams of the hinterland of Milan like Lecco, Como and Pavia). In the second place, for the first time we have seen the appearance of an Ultra movement supporting the national team – an anomaly if you only think that in preceding decades the Italian national team has always been immune to Ultra fans. Now there has in fact appeared a movement – the 'Ultras Italia' – which is of a quintessentially

---

9 A neo-fascist and an admirer of Himmler, Franco Freda was given a 15-year sentence for subversion.

nationalist and xenophobic character. Their first appearance was at Parma when 400/500 Ultras Italia attended the Italy's last World Cup qualifying match. They followed the orders (concerning position on the terraces, chants and banners) of a small group of leaders wearing Forza Nuova T-shirts.

Perhaps the explanation for this change should be sought outside the stadiums and identified in those social processes which have for sometime been changing Italian society. It is thus possible, perhaps, to see in these new nationalist, racist and xenophobic attitudes in the Ultra movement an effect of what we can call, following Norbert Elias, a more general process of 'de-civilization'. Indeed it seems to me that our society, our cities, the places in which we live our social life, are being de-civilized. We are seeing a weakening of those control mechanisms, external and internal, which control passions, perceptions of others and living together. We live today, to use a fashionable term, in a 'risk society'. And risk gives rise to fear. Fear in turn gives rise to alarm and anxiety. Alarm and anxiety can remain undefined sensations, abstract, deprived of an object that can be identified as a cause. But sometimes they can change – indeed they demand to be changed – into concrete sensations – of hate, of rejection, of aversion – for something or someone in particular.

This, I fear, is what the extreme right groups in Italian stadiums, with greater or lesser degrees of success, are trying to do. Provide young Ultras with an object onto which they can channel their fears and anxieties, whether it be the fan of an opposing team or a black player. And it is easy to get young people, increasingly deprived of alternative sources of places to meet and of a strong sense of belonging, to make this step. A few little ploys will do. For example, take the insults which are now routinely directed at the black players who play in Italy. All you need to do is get all the whole curva to insult one of the players on the opposing team – and then – and this is the second step – to get them to insult him because he is black. A simple way to plant the seeds of a racism that can quickly reproduce itself.

3. The iconography of Ultra sites

I have good reasons, therefore, as an ex-fan, for being depressed. And still more when I happen to visit the websites that almost all the Ultra groups have put on the web.[10] What do these sites in fact contain and what do they want to communicate? The thing that strikes me most every time I see them appear on the screen of my computer is how faithfully they mirror the way in which

---

10 A good point of departure for visiting many of these sites is the collection of links available at http://www.ultralodigiani.org/collegamenti.htm#I [accessed 27 June 2007 (translator)].

the world of the Ultras has changed and how it has lost all contact with its own roots as a movement of young fans. Browsing attentively you become immediately aware of how they are a vehicle for a plurality of messages and how they are constructed using various communicative registers, indeed quite skilfully; but what is also evident is how most of the messages they contain now only amount to an exaltation of violence and propaganda for extreme right and racist political positions. Naturally this impression is not valid for all Ultra sites. For this reason I always try to focus above all on three elements which are pivotal to the strategies of self-representation adopted by each group and the contents they want to communicate. These elements are: 1) graphics and logos, 2) photographs and videos, and 3) the so-called 'wall'. But when I put them together and browse them in succession I cannot help thinking that the result produced by the combination of these elements is none other than to create a repeated ceremony of self-degradation, an insistent representation of their own collective identity, not as positive or even exalting as the Ultras would wish, but on the contrary as poor and vulgar.

I shall now try to illustrate these elements one by one in order to try to give a general idea of what these sites contain beginning with their images and logos, which usually form the supporting columns of every Ultra site given that this element concerns the emblem, the photos and the history of each group – in other words, the most significant elements with which each Ultra group represents itself to the external world, that is to say, to other fans, and internally, to its own members. There is something that is noticed immediately: not all Ultra sites have the same format. There are many differences between them and the most important certainly concerns whether or not they want to highlight the icons which manifest their political loyalties. Left-leaning groups usually have fewer problems about expressing their ideas and displaying their emblems while Ultra groups with right-wing sympathies are often very reluctant to exhibit their symbols. The iconography of the left, with the image of 'Che' Guevara in prime position, is present, for example, on the sites of Empoli's Rangers and Perugia's Ingrifati. It is more difficult to find explicit right-wing symbolism on the sites which refer to this political area. Lazio's Irriducibili, Torino's Granata Korps and Roma's Boys, to mention but a few, have always been recognized as right-wing groups, indeed extreme right groups, and yet on their websites no symbols – like celtic crosses or swastikas – are displayed which explicitly refer to this ideology, though celtic crosses and swastikas are openly exhibited on banners and flags every Sunday on the terraces in the stadium. This is a reluctance that can be explained by the law which prohibits the public exhibition of symbols of a Nazi, fascist, anti-Semitic or xenophobic matrix and the obvious desire not to incur penal sanctions. All in all, however, it can be said that if sites are left-aligned they make full use of images and logos which call upon a consolidated left-wing iconography, while sites which are on the right make use instead of phrases and slogans which draw upon the fascist right – I have already mentioned some; I add here some other examples: 'Our honour is called loyalty'; 'Honour and fidelity' – and above all graphics which make use of black backgrounds, the Italian flags and runic letters.[11]

In this context, though it may seem odd, we also find online commerce in materials, though not all groups are engaged in this. A standard Ultra website almost always contains a section called 'Materials' consisting of photos of merchandise of various kinds, prices and information about how to order. This section is often indispensable given that Ultra groups have always financed themselves selling their own merchandise (scarves, hats, stickers with the logo of the group and so on) and the Internet represents a shop window that they cannot ignore, above all in the case of those teams which have fans all over Italy. Only the Roma Ultras form an exception to the rule in that though they publish images of their material, they do not sell online and invite those who are interested to buy their materials directly from group members at the stadium, perhaps to encourage direct contacts with their members and supporters rather than limiting themselves to a simple and cold form of distance selling. Among the other services which Ultra sites offer, there is the possibility of downloading backgrounds and screensavers for your computer and Ultra choruses in MP3 format. Bologna's Vecchia Guardia,[12] for example, only offer a few backgrounds but they are of high quality. If you are looking for MP3 format football chants I would recommend the sites of Milan's Fossa dei Leoni and Lazio's Irriducibili.[13]

But let's turn to the photographs and the videos, the real pride and joy of many Ultra sites. In this section, often called rather affectedly 'Art Gallery', you can find a display of the photos of the group's best choreographed displays, of their biggest turnouts, of their most original banners – in practice

---

11 Antonio Roversi, the author of this book, suggested visiting the site of Palermo's Warriors which was last available at http://www.imd.it/warriors/html/italiano.htm for an example of right-wing iconography. The site has since disappeared, probably as a consequence of the killing of a police officer, Filippo Raciti after the Palermo-Catania derby of 2 February 2007 played at Stadio Angelo Massimino, in Catania. Raciti was killed when Catania Ultras attacked the police during a riot after the match. Raciti's death, which brought all Italian football matches, even those of the national team, to be suspended for a week, caused strong emotion in Italy, with a great and somewhat uncommon amount of solidarity towards the Italian law enforcement forces (translator's note).

12 The website of Bologna's Vecchia Guardia is available at http://vecchiaguardia.tifonet. it/ [accessed 27 June 2007 (translator)].

13 The Irriducibili website is available at http://www.Irriducibili.com/prima.html; the Fossa dei Leoni website is still available at http://www.fdl.it but carries a notice announcing its imminent closure [both accessed 27 June 2007 (translator)].

of anything which serves to communicate the greatness of the group. This part of the site, dedicated to self-celebration, is accessible to anyone, both supporters and enemies. There are, however, differences between sites in this respect, too. Some sites only display photos of their own fans, while others show pictures of enemy fans, usually to denigrate or insult them. But the main difference remains that concerning scenes of violence. Images of clashes inside and outside the stadium, or of violent banners with racist and xenophobic messages, are often found on the sites of the most extreme groups because they want to transmit a strong, well-defined image of their group. Lazio's Irriducibili, a group considered to be one of the most fearsome on the Italian Ultra scene, is a good example in this respect. In their archive they publish images of banners with racist and xenophobic messages ('A team of niggers, a curva of Jews') and threats to those who govern football in Italy ('A play-off or war') and of clashes with the police.[14] Apart from ensuring them the limelight in the Ultra world, these images serve, above all, to consolidate an image of the group as united in ideas and committed to extremist actions. Atlanta's Wild Kaos, to mention another example, has adopted the same strategy and publishes images of brawls with enemy fans on its website, again with the same objective of representing itself as a violent group that is always ready for a physical confrontation.[15]

This may seem a very simple form of communication, one which pursues its objective using images of powerful visual impact. However, I believe that it would be reductive to see it only in these terms. It may seem like a monotonous reinterpretation of the same theme in which only the subjects change and which repeats itself like a maniacal, obsessive litany on every site, but it seems to me that it in fact pursues an objective that is more wide ranging: that of evoking a symbolic universe in which a unique element reigns supreme – physical violence exhibited as a positive, shared value. I have always been very sceptical of journalistic accounts of the Ultra movement which offer nothing more that a repeated rant on the hordes of violent, drunk barbarians who have come out of who knows what cave and who deserve a life sentence if not the death penalty. I get the impression that I'm reading a second-rate version of Gustave Le Bon's *The Crowd: A Study of the Popular Mind*[16] seasoned with ingredients taken from Lombroso. But it seems to me that the Ultra movement has always been the bearer of a 'strong' culture capable of transforming the terraces into a social space in which, despite differences of social origin, of motivation, of subjective stimuli, of styles

14 See http://www.Irriducibili.com/prima.html.

15 The Wild Kaos website is available at http://wildkaos.tifonet.it/ [accessed 27 June 2007 (translator)].

16 Available on line at the Project Guttenberg site http://www.gutenberg.org/etext/445 [accessed 27 June 2007 (translator)].

of life and diverse political convictions, certain norms and certain rules are valid for all. These norms and these rules have changed over time, but one has remained constant and is accepted by all: violence as a positive value, as something to nurture and practice, that is capable of conferring more power and prestige the more that it is nurtured and practiced. It is this message, beyond the self-celebration, that many Ultra sites promote every day via the web for a vast public of young people. And it is here, in my opinion, that the real problem lies. Because if it is true that Ultra groups are responsible for acts of violence, vandalism and brutality towards anyone who happens to stray into their path, it is equally true that it is very reductive to measure how socially dangerous they are only on the basis of the penal code. The real danger that they represent lies rather in their being propagators, not only through actions but by means of a wide range of communicative strategies, in which their websites play a not unimportant part, of a message that is the contrary of every rule of civil existence, namely that conflicts between groups and individuals can only be resolved with an iron bar, by physically attacking the enemy and wearing the emblems of those political cultures – or if you prefer, of ideologies – which historically have most preached and practiced contempt for, and rejection, and even annihilation, of those other than yourself. And it is a message that does not only refer to behaviour in the stadium but an incitement to action that concerns the ordinary lives of all fans, Ultras and those who are not, beyond the limits of Sunday.

Here is another example that leaves no doubt about the matter: http://cimelidiguerra.tifonet.it.[17] The name of this site means 'relics of war'. The heading on the homepage has something of the nature of a challenge about it: 'This site limits itself to photographing a phenomenon, that of the Ultra movement, which already exists, and has no intention of encouraging anyone to commit uncivil or criminal actions which could damage public property or that of others and ... BLA ... BLA ... BLA!!' And a little below we find 'this site was created to show our younger visitors the feats of their forefathers (sic!) and to enable the latter to relive the emotions they experienced when young'. On this site, apart from photographs of Adolf Hitler, Leon Degrelle, Rudolf Hess, the Hitler Youth, of members of White Power and of Forza Nuova banners, it is possible to download any number of videos which show every sort of civil disorder: clashes between opposing fans, confrontations with the police, fights in the street. The strong point of this site, however, is the section entitled 'Stolen banners', that is to say the war relics to which the name of the site refers. In a caption the webmaster explains, 'One of the classic actions of what has been called 'the Ultra subculture' is the theft of the opponent's banner. Stealing the banner of the opposing fans, better

---

17 Available as of 27 June 2007 (translator's note).

if that of the Ultras, is a clear insult comparable to the theft of the enemy's flag in war. You can understand why in 30 years several hundred have been stolen'. Following this explanation we find page after page in which are listed, rigorously in alphabetical order and with many photographs as proof, all the Ultra groups who have exhibited banners on the terraces taken from adversaries in ways that certainly were not peaceful.

4. Keyboard Ultras

Supporting your team = War. Simple, clear, something everybody can understand. This is the message that is transmitted by a site of this kind. I could cite many others which mirror the content of this one but it would be an unnecessary waste of paper. Also because at this point the problem should be glaringly obvious in all its ugliness. Who are these sites directed at? Clearly at an audience of young people, as I have said. But which young people? The webmaster of 'War Relics' is right to address the young people of today, because the Ultras of yesterday, the Ultras of 10 or 20 years ago were not 'forefathers' and were different to what he imagines them to have been. They preached and practiced the use of physical violence but it was a violence that had its own codes. It was a violence that had precise rules that all the Ultras knew and respected. You only fought other groups of Ultras. You did not fight the police. 'Civilians', that is to say, ordinary fans, should not be involved. You don't commit acts of vandalism against people or things. Nothing should be done that has not been decided and accepted by all. Above all, there was a limit to the use of physical violence. You could use your hands, sometimes sticks, nothing else. Someone who did not respect these rules was not an Ultra. He was contemptible and was immediately banished from the stadium and rendered innocuous. In other words, the older, more experienced Ultras exercised control over the younger ones. And they did not much like publicity. The violence in the stadium was for them a private business, a way to settle accounts inside their world. Everything changed, however, when a different kind of Ultra appeared, the so-called 'three hour Ultras', very young fans who arrived on the terraces for the most part attracted by the fame of hardness that surrounded the Ultra groups, a fame that had reached them through many public communication channels, not least television programmes and specialized magazines.[18] These Ultras were not in the least interested in the 'football culture' of those who had preceded them. For them it was all reduced to the ostentatious exhibition of the group's 'coat of arms' and the desire to experience, without delay, the

---

18 Like the famous and historic *Supertifo* magazine and other rather less successful like *Hooligans*.

thrill of a clash with the adversary. This was a generation that represented an almost irreparable break with that which preceded it and which gradually took its place. And it brought a stadium mentality to the terraces that radically changed the rules of the game, mostly importantly rules concerning the use of physical violence, which in effect were abolished.

The situation got even worse when the 'three hour Ultra' was joined by another figure, that of the 'keyboard Ultra'. This is the figure that is rampant on the web today in the so-called wall section of Ultra websites. walls are a sort of notice board where anyone can write what he wants and which originally were intended as a meeting place where Ultras could talk amongst themselves and express opinions about the footballing fortunes of their team. However the wall has long lost this characteristic and become something else. And since it is my job to document a reality which few outside the world of the Ultras know at first hand, I feel obliged, with reluctance, apologizing in advance, to present a small sample chosen by chance of what you can read in these sections:

(On Florentina's Curva Fiesole Wall): "you are nothing but loathsome dirt. I would make you swallow castor oil all day beat you all the way into an extermination camp!!!"[19]

(On Mantova's Fighters Wall): "I would insult you all evening but it's not worth the effort. ... ciao shit".[20]

(On the Wall of the Ultras Inside website): "sampdoriani and fiorentini you are only bastards full of shit always and only onwards genoa!!!!!!" "7 February is approaching ... Milanisti we are waiting for you!!!!!!!!!! We are the real Ultras!!!!!!!!! Napoletani go and sell tomatoes, ok? Your mother is a whore on the coast".[21]

(On the Roma Ultras Wall): "If you want to drink real blood drink black-and-white blood", "We massacre every Inter supporter we catch".[22]

But the most visited wall is that of the site of the whole Ultra movement, Tifo-net.[23] I reproduce here what I read on the site one day chosen by chance in March 2005:

- We all wipe our arses with those Bologna Ultras shits
- You've pissed us off.

---

19 http://muro.tifonet.it/index.php?cod_muro=13&azione=send.

20 http://tifonet.it/fighters/muro/.

21 http://www.ultrasinside.it/.

22 http://www.asromaultras.it/scritte.html.

23 http://www.muro.tifonet.it/.

- massesi pathetic wankers
- nobody fears you, no one respects you ... BUGGER YOU NAPOLETANO!!! It's not that you hate all of Italy, it's the boot that's disgusted with you
- DUX MEA LUX[24]
- CAGLIARI RULES!! DIRTY BASTARDS YOU SIDE WITH THE POLICE. MILANO SHIT
- LIVORNESI??? DON'T YOU REMEMBER THE BEATING YOU GOT AT PISA? OR HOW YOU RAN AWAY WITH YOUR TAILS BETWEEN YOUR LEGS BY THE SEA? YOU'RE YELLOWER THAN TOSCANA AND YOU ALWAYS WANT TO SHOUT YOUR MOUTH OFF X TO FEEL LIKE YOU'RE SOMEBODY....YOU'RE PATHETIC. GO FUCK YOURSELVES.....THE ONLY ONES WHO CAN TALK OF FIGHTING ARE THE FIORENTINI (SHITS), CARRARINI, US PISANI AND THE PISTOIESI (PEASANTS). SCONVOLTS PISA AND THATS ALL
- chieti you make a prick vomit, I'm from ripa teatina and I support ripa. You make us shit.
- DI CANIO WE'RE GOING TO BRAIN YOU
- LETS BURN LIVORNO.....!!! LIVORNO IN FLAMES....!!!!
- pescarese wanker!
- You've just got into A and you piss everyone off, you want to fuck everyone and everything...just bugger off, we'll talk about in a couple of years
- LAZIALI AND GIALLOZZOZZI YOUR INFAMY IS THE RUIN OF OUR ULTRA WORLD
- TODAY FERILLI AND ILARY AND SENSI'S DAUGHTER,WILL BE ON THE RING ROAD LOOKING FOR CUSTOMERS TO COLLECT MONEY TO PAY THE FINES AND POSSIBLY TO SCRAPE TOGETHER THE MONEY FOR THE AWAY GAME AT FIRENZE, NERO COME BACK AND LIGHT THE FLARES IN ROME!! FIRENZE HATES YOU.
- Verona = Romanian homeland NAPOLI VOMITS ON YOU. Juliet was a WHORE
- lecce shit leccesi full of shit!!!!!!!!!!!!
- RIMINESI SHITTY PRICKHEADS!!!!
- bari shit bari shit bari shit bari shit bari shit
- COME ON TORRES!!!!!!!!!!!!!! CAGLIARI SHITS
- STEFANO RICCI BASTARD AND COWARD
- alessandro pietrini bastard
- BASTARD SASSARESE WATCH YOUR ARSES WE'RE GOING TO BUGGER YOU!!! SPEZIA ULTRAS RULE
- IN FOGGIA I SCREWED A FOGGIA WANKER FOR 100 EUROS

And so on. As you can see, it is an anthology of insults, threats, obscene phrases, swearwords, and abuse which reminds me of that phenomenon typical of chatrooms and newsrooms which goes by the name of 'flame'. 'Flaming' on the web means acting in an arrogant, offensive or even hostile way towards other users. And it is a phenomenon that is quite widespread,

---

24 Macaronic Latin for 'Mussolini (Il Duce) is my shining light' (translator's note).

as is evident if you spend some hours in any digital environment which is used by a large number of users. At regular intervals it is almost inevitable that you see swearwords or offensive expressions flowing across the screen, with obscenities repeated obsessively, without any apparent purpose. Their authors are often very young users who, having little or nothing to say, can find no better way to show that 'we exist too' than resorting to useless vulgarity. But walls also remind me of an experiment conducted some years ago by Radio Radicale. Radio Radicale transmitted a programme that was re-baptized 'Radio Parolaccia' (Radio Swearword) which everyone could telephone and say what they wanted without being censured. In other words, their microphones were open to anyone. The result was a succession of profanities, swearwords, obscenities, blasphemies broadcast live. Radio Radicale became a ring for verbal confrontations between rival football supporters who made appointments with each other. Though the medium is different, it seems to me that the space once occupied by Radio Parolaccia is now occupied by the various walls. Visiting them you find the same phrases, the same expressions and the same outpourings that were heard in that radio transmission. Insults and provocations, tit-for-tat between opposing factions, racist and xenophobic invectives, threats at a personal level naming names, appointments for physical confrontations, provocative images, contempt for the dead – this and much else is what you find on walls.

However, for the sake of accuracy, I believe that I should add that this verbal violence is not to blame when violence does occur involving Ultra groups. The Ultras themselves don't put great store in the messages published on walls. And, if I can add another consideration, it seems to me that since this communicative space came into existence, the role that the so-called 'keyboard Ultras' have created for themselves has not been other than to create confusion and conflict in a world that was already in any case complicated and fractured. It is necessary, therefore, to be cautious about what you read on walls and not to believe everything you read there. If these messages have a significance it lies rather on a more general level, in constituting documentary proof of the level of degradation that the contemporary Ultra movement has sunk to as a whole. I call it degradation because that is what it is from a strictly sociological point of view, but perhaps it would be more appropriate to define it as aphasia. Young people who spend their time writing messages in repetitive fashion like those I quoted earlier from a wall in fact speak a language of nothing. Their words are empty simulacra which mirror a cultural absence, perhaps even an absence of a deviant subculture.[25] In other words, though posing as rebels, as different, anti-system, they show that they have nothing to share even with a world of deviance and marginalization

---

25 On the concept of 'subculture' see the classic text by D. Hebdige (1979), *Subculture and the Meaning of Style* (London: Methuen).

and its symbolic and linguistic codes. They lack social membership and any critical capacity and are only able to ape, in way that is almost Pavlovian, what they have seen others do or try. The result, sadly, is that rotting mass of vulgar slogans which I reproduced above. Nothing else.

What is there to say in conclusion about this panoramic view of Ultra sites? Very simply, that in my opinion, you can understand much more about Italian Ultras by visiting their websites with a certain regularity than by spending an entire season on the terraces with them. Indeed, if read attentively, their webpages render transparent those linguistic codes and symbolic references which are transferred to the terraces every Sunday and often to places outside the stadium. Take their political symbolism and their exhibition of flags and banners with Celtic crosses, runic axes and swastikas. For how long was it argued that this exhibition had nothing to do with extremist politics but was only a symbolic mode of reinforcing the image of toughness and brutality which these groups wanted to promote of themselves? Or take the television talk show which every time some particularly serious episode of football violence occurs, collects together a handful of politicians, federation executives and journalists who, 35 years after the appearance of this movement in our country, are incapable of going beyond a useless recreation of the stereotype according to which Ultras are hooligans and delinquents.[26] An afternoon spent browsing these sites, on the other hand, and all this nonsense is revealed for what it is. The fruit of an incapacity to see what is really happening in a part of the world of the young people of today which has always made of its separateness a *raison d'être* and a distinctive characteristic. These sites in fact show us how this separateness is intertwined today more than ever with certain deep currents which run transversally through our society, and how it is contaminated by them, producing results which are more far more dangerous than clashes with the police or rival fans, or the looting of a motorway café. For this reason I hope that I have illustrated the nature of the phenomenon with the clarity necessary to bring this home, but I will summarise my findings once again so as not to run the risk of being misinterpreted. These sites are a shop window in which are displayed all the ingredients of a social peril that consists firstly in the repeated and almost obsessive promotion of the idea that violence is always good, beautiful and to be valued; secondly in the integration of this idea of violence as a positive value in a more general extreme right perspective with all the normative corollaries and practical ties that follow from this; and finally in the degradation of the communicative capacities of subjects who are psychologically and culturally vulnerable and to the point that their attempts at polemic amount to mere vulgarity.

---

26 Useless, obviously, from the point of view of understanding the phenomenon. However, I have strong doubts as to whether this is useful from any point of view.

If you think that every Sunday tens of thousands of young people absorb in bigger or smaller doses this mixture of ingredients promoted in various ways on the terraces by Ultras all over Italy, I really believe that there is little reason to celebrate the 'immanence' of the Internet in this regard.

Chapter 3

The Black Pages:
Fascist and Neo-Nazi Websites

1. An avowal, a skinhead dance and an evening at the discotheque

In 1995 I carried out some research on a group of young Nazi skinheads (or 'naziskin', as they are better known in Italy) in a big city in the North.[1] I can't say what the group was called but the city was Milan. I spent a great deal of time with them, usually in the evenings. In the mornings and the afternoons these young neo-Nazis were occupied with their own affairs. Some of them studied, some of them worked. Only in the evening at around about seven o'clock did they meet up in a bar where they usually remained until midnight. All that time was spent in various activities which I carefully recorded in my research notes. I had many conversations with them, which were often informal and spontaneous, but on other occasions – in accordance with the protocols of empirical research – I interviewed them following a structure I had diligently prepared beforehand. I also collected various materials of a documentary kind. Magazines, fanzines, photographs, leaflets, videos, and numerous CDs of Oi! and RAC music produced by both Italian and foreign bands of the far right.[2] I believe that I must be one of the few non-Nazis to possess such a good collection of music of this kind.

I began thinking about doing research on naziskins two years before this, when I read in the papers about what had happened in a city in Northern Germany. That city was called Rostock, and a hostel of Vietnamese immigrants had been set on fire there. In the months which followed there were other analogous episodes: at Moelnn a Turkish woman and two

---

1   From here on the Italian term, 'naziskin' will be used in this text. Like many 'borrowed' words in Italian (it is obviously derived from 'Nazi skinhead'), 'naziskin' is an invariable noun (it has the same form in the plural and the singular), but as this can sound odd in English I have decided to give it a plural form ending in 's' (translator's note).

2   The most loved music style in the skinhead movement is a working-class street-level subgenre of punk rock that originated in the United Kingdom in the 1970s known as Oi! RAC is the acronym of Rock against Communism which was a series of white power rock music concerts that started in the United Kingdom in the late 1970s, and has become the name for the associated music genre. For more on this see Marchi, V. (1997), *Nazi-Rock. Pop music e Destra radicale* (Roma: Castelvecchi).

children died in the flames of their house; three children and two Turkish women died in the blaze of their home at Sollingen. These were tragic events but they could seem to have been accidental or the work of a madman. In reality – as we shall see – things had happened differently. These episodes were a signal that the past was returning. Underground things were stirring: limited initiatives, small scale aggregations, rediscoveries of something that many, if not all, had considered buried under the dust of years but that was coming back in to the light to reclaim a place in public life. But it was a signal that was not easy to discern. Above all from a distance. In Italy, right wing extremists had put in an appearance in the past. In the '60s there were the 'picchiatori': thugs with extreme right sympathies, the offspring of a fascist lumpenproletariat that had fed on the worst consequences of the economic boom that was changing the face of Italy. In the '70s it was the turn of the 'pariolini' (neo-fascists named after a quarter in Rome) and the 'snababilini' (Milanese neo-fascists named after a quarter in Milan), young people from the right side of the tracks in Rome and Milan who mixed a nostalgic itch, a predisposition to violence and above all a misunderstood condition of social privilege with a culture of arrogance and bullying which exploded in all its ferocity – emblematically – in the Circeo slaughter.[3] Long ago events, however, which belonged to a story that we thought over and finished with. True, you could still see some fascists once a year at Predappio (Benito Mussolini's birthplace), participating in a ritual consisting in stiff arm salutes and nostalgic songs. But all in all, it seemed like water under the bridge of Italian society, water that was drying up in the tiny rivulets where it had ended up. But things were not quite like that. That past had not evaporated without trace. Though reduced to a thin stream there was water enough to provide some sustenance and some seeds could grow. Seeds that seemed different at first sight but which fed on the same substances, on the same memories and on the same ambitions which continued to ferment in that water. And which in the end produced the last figure in the pack: those skinheads of the far-right commonly known as naziskins.[4]

---

3   On the evening of 30 September 1975 three young neo-fascists, Angelo Izzo, Gianni Guido and Andrea Ghira invited two girls, Maria Rosaria Lopez and Donatella Colasanti to a party at Ghira's villa at Circeo and there they abused and tortured them, leaving them for dead. Maria Rosaria Lopez died but Donatella Colasanti survived, though in a terrible state, by pretending to be dead.

4   For more on Nazi skinheads and naziskins see the following texts: Blondet, M. (1993), *I nuovi barbari. Gli skinheads parlano* (Milano: Effedieffe); Cadalanu, G. (1994), *Skinheads. Dalla musica giamaicana al saluto romano* (Lecce: Argo); Castellani, A. (1994), *Senza chioma nè legge. Skins italiani* (Roma: Manifestolibri); Hasselbach, I. (1996), *Fuhrer-Ex: Memoirs of a Former Neo-Nazi* (New York: Random House); Marchi, V. (1993), *Blood and Honour. Rapporto internazionale sulla destra skinhead* (Rome: Koinè).

It took me a long time to manage to get into contact with that group, perhaps the largest on the Italian scene at the time. The problem was resolved by a stroke of luck. I met someone who knew someone who knew someone else. The latter was a gatekeeper who managed to fix an appointment for me with some naziskins in a bar in piazza Napoli in Milan.[5] Of that first meeting, apart from the tension, and, let's be honest, the fear that I felt, I particularly remember something else. I don't know whether my reader is familiar with the kind of T-shirts which are produced for the tour of a singer or a band. Usually there is an image on the front that depicts the singer or the band or a logo or a particular symbol. The image produced for a Rolling Stones tour in which a large red tongue sticks out of a crimson mouth is famous. On the back are printed the places and dates of the concerts. For example: New York – 18 May 2005, London – 22 May 2005, Madrid – 26 May 2005, and so on. Well, leaning on the door frame of the entrance to the bar that evening was a youngster wearing a version of that kind of T-shirt which was rather unusual. On the front there was an image of Hitler with the words 'Adolf Hitler. European Tour 1939 – 45' printed below it. On the back there was written something like: Poland – 1939, Belgium – 1940, France – 1941, Denmark – 1942 and so on. In other words, it bore the names of the countries occupied by the armies of the Third Reich and the dates when they were invaded. In a certain sense it was a fascinating T-shirt. Certainly an unusual one. It drew the attention of all like a magnet and it could be guaranteed to provoke a reaction. And yet the young man wearing it was completely at his ease and wore it with the same naturalness with which I wore my anonymous shirt.

Though I collected a great deal of material I have never published a book on that research. Only a couple of articles in a sociology journal. When I finished my investigations and I had left the 'setting', I found it difficult to re-acquire quickly the detachment necessary for relating and analysing that experience. I tried again later but every time that I took up that material again and I returned in memory to those places, and people and to the discourses and events which I had witnessed, I was overwhelmed by such a feeling of rejection that I immediately closed my notebook and tried to think of something else. I shall give only three short examples of the things that I saw and heard long ago in 1995. The first concerns a declaration made during a chat. The others are two episodes which occurred while I was physically present.

One evening I was talking to one of the leaders. There were in fact three leaders in that naziskin group. There was a political leader – the most important and most respected – who made the decisions in decisive moments

---

5   The gatekeeper or doorman is someone who thanks to his contacts and influence is able to fix up a researcher with his first meeting with the people or groups he wants to study. The first step in sociological research of this kind is to identify the gatekeeper.

and represented the group in relations with other Italian or foreign neo-Nazi organizations. There was the head of the organization who had the job of maintaining the cohesion of the group, selecting new adherents and dealing with all the logistic and economic aspects. Finally there was the military chief who had the job of organizing security and training members in one-to-one combat and street fighting (for example in the case of a demonstration or a punitive expedition) at a paramilitary camp situated in a relatively isolated part of Liguria. Well, as I was saying, one evening I was talking to one of the leaders – the political leader. I wanted to know how come young people barely more than twenty years old spent all their free time always together, without contact with other people, closed in their own claustrophobic world. Without ever going to the cinema, dancing in a discotheque, spending time alone with their girl friend, or – I don't know what – playing football or doing something stupid. Instead, only meeting up every day with the 'camerati' (the fascist term for 'comrades') and drinking an incredible amount of beer. I approached the question in a roundabout way, talking of some of the activists that I had got to know and expressing some general judgments of a superficial kind. He seemed irritated by the conversation. It was evident that it annoyed him that someone should talk in these terms of people who were very important to him. So he started to give me a lesson on the significance of 'cameratismo' (the fascist term for 'comradeship') and on its importance in the life of all of us. 'And if someone betrays you, if he goes over to the other side or denounces you all, what would you do?' I asked him at a certain point. He looked me straight in the eyes and said only four words: 'I would kill him'. And then, after a pause, he added: 'We are at war and in war martial law operates. Traitors and spies are shot'. He wasn't joking. He was talking seriously and with conviction.

The first episode that I want to relate concerns a scene that I witnessed one evening in a bar in Milan. The naziskins had moved on to the bar after abandoning piazza Napoli. That evening, as almost every evening for that matter, the atmosphere was tranquil. Fifteen or so naziskins were chatting here and there: some leaning on the bar, others seated around tables. Suddenly a person entered. He was a middle-aged man, modestly dressed. He was clearly drunk. He was unsteady on his feet as he approached the bar and murmured incomprehensible phrases to himself. He asked for a drink. He began to sip a glass of wine and then he looked around him. He seemed to suddenly become aware of the presence of other people. Those strange young people attracted his attention. Above all he seemed to notice the badges that some of them wore sewn on to the sleeves of their military jackets. Celtic crosses. The sight of them was like an electric shock. He began to get agitated and to say things which became increasingly clear. He let rip. 'Fucking fascists', he began to shout, 'Fucking fascists … I fought in the Resistance'. He addressed nobody in particular. He shouted it at the room. It seemed almost as though his alcohol fogged mind had been cleared by a flash of light. A flash that had carried him back in time and space. I watched him, but, as always happens to me when I sense danger, the only thing I felt at that moment was fear. My hands began to tremble slightly. I had a cold sensation in my stomach as though I had swallowed ice. My legs had become as heavy as concrete and I couldn't move my feet. Then there happened what had to happen. Three or four of the young men got up, walked towards him and surrounded him. One of them grabbed him by the collar and in a hiss asked him something like 'What did you say? Eh? What did you say you bastard?' They dragged him out by the jacket and with a push they made him fall onto the pavement. I thought that it was over, perhaps to reassure myself. But it was not over. In five or six they circled him and began kicking him. On the ground, the man protected himself as best he could but he was hit everywhere. Kicks to the spine, the head, the legs. One naziskin, with his heavy Doc Martins, stamped on his hands several times. The man's cries became weaker. How long did that scene last? Probably no more than a minute or two, but to me it seemed like an eternity. The youths came back in and one of them said to me laughing: 'Do you know what we call this? The dance of the skin'.

Second episode. One day I was informed that a famous English Oi! band would soon be giving a concert in a discotheque in the Pordenone district. The naziskins proposed that I go with them and I accepted the invitation. I didn't know that band – just as I knew next to nothing of Oi! music – but the opportunity seemed too tempting to miss. The event was so important that the arrival of groups of naziskins from all over Italy was predicted and it was a good chance for me to widen my horizons about a world that had been unknown to me until a few months previously. I had them give me directions about how to reach the concert venue – I have kept the leaflet with the instructions which was distributed to all those who wanted to go – and on the date and time stipulated I presented myself at the entrance of what seemed a large discotheque situated in the periphery of a small Northern city. It is a habit of mine – or better a defect – to always arrive early for appointments and that is what happened on this occasion. The time given had been nine in the evening and at nine on the dot I was already there. There weren't many people there yet. I noticed, however, a large coach with Yugoslavian number plates, indicating that the Ustashi had also arrived from nearby Croatia. I looked around and when I saw that people – apparently all naziskins – were starting to go in, I bought a ticket and entered too. An error. Entering so quickly I didn't noticed what was going on outside – but thanks to my precipitateness I got to see what was anything but a simple concert. Once inside I found myself inside a very big room. Completely empty if you excluded the stage already set up for the band at the end of the room with lots of Nazi flags, and a bar for drinks near the entrance. Slowly the discotheque began to fill up. At a rough guess I would say that there were about five or six hundred people when the band came on stage. When the musicians appeared all hell broke loose. The audience all started shouting Nazi slogans and giving the Roman salute and jumping in the air. Once the roar and the shouting had ceased the guitarist struck the first cord. And what had before seemed an unbearable noise was nothing compared to the acoustic explosion of three guitars with amplifiers on maximum. I don't think that more than ten seconds had passed before I was completely deaf and also a bit stunned. I couldn't hear anything any more except an avalanche of sound that penetrated my ears and seemed to reverberate in my stomach. In the hope of getting a grip on myself I went to the bar and ordered something to drink. While I sipped my drink I looked around me and observed the scene. In the centre of the room a large number of naziskins were engaged in what is – inaccurately – called a dance. In reality it was the pogo: jumping up and down, pushing, thrashing around as if miming a brawl. Indeed the pogo is just that: an enactment of a brawl to music. At first sight it seems like a brawl but it isn't. Although it looks like a violent scuffle between hostile people, in fact it involves thrashing your body about in a wild way according to precise rules. And the first rule is that if someone should fall to the ground those around him should move away to enable him to get up and ensure that he is not trampled on by the other 'dancers'. But beyond the stupefaction provoked by that spectacle, I noticed something else. There was a continuous, edgy milling of naziskins who were not dancing at the bottom of the room to the right of the bar. The discotheque was lit only in the area of the stage and the further you went towards the exit the more you were immersed in semi-darkness. I couldn't make out what was happening. I could only see people moving tensely back and forth, an agitated coming and going for which I could find no explanation. I was straining my eyes in the effort to distinguish something in that semi-darkness when a naziskin I knew passed in front of me. I greeted him with a wave of the hand but he did not reply. Then he went back to where he had come from. I grabbed him by the arm and with all the breath I could muster I yelled in his ear: 'Is there something wrong?' In his turn he shouted into my ear: 'The filth have come'. That then was the reason for so much agitation. A sizeable group of Sharps – left wing skinheads – had arrived and all that movement was the prelude to what would inevitably happen.[6] While he quickly moved away from me I noticed that he had a chain in his hand. A moment later a situation was created that it is difficult to describe. I'll try all the same. So: on the stage an Oi! band playing unbearable music that deafened you beyond measure. In the centre of the room a few

6   Sharp is the acronym of Skinhead Against Racial Prejudice.

hundred naziskins pogoing like people possessed in mystic neo-Nazi ecstasy, totally out of their heads by this point. And at the bottom of the room, on the right and in the semi-darkness, another hundred or so skins, more or less equally divided between the neo-Nazis and far left varieties, attacking each other with chains, knuckle-dusters, studded belts, baseball bats and – I fear – knives. Perhaps infected by the atmosphere I thought that for once the spectacle was worth the price of the ticket. The fight, the real one, lasted quite a long time, five or ten minutes, I would say. The two fronts took turns to fling themselves unsparingly against their adversaries. Several people fell to the ground and remained there. There were wounded people who were bleeding and who were carried out of the room. Then it stopped. I think because the Sharps had gone. The band, unaware of what had happened, or perhaps not, had continued playing the whole time and did not seem to have any intention of stopping for at least two hours. The dancers had continued to pogo hell for leather, indifferent to what was happening behind them. The hard guys had played their favourite game. Everyone would return home satisfied. I realized that I had finished my drink. I ordered another and gulped it down. I drew a deep breath and then another and then yet another. My heart had stopped galloping. I could go home now. It had certainly been an unforgettable night.

2. Fascist websites

I have related these episodes because when I began visiting Italian extreme right websites I expected to return to that same atmosphere saturated with physical violence which I had breathed in the course of that now distant research. Instead, except in some cases about which I will have something more to say further on, I realized that this fear was unfounded. As far as I can see, the Italian websites of the extreme right are in fact rather different from, for example, the American and German varieties. I will attempt to demonstrate this in a minute when I make a comparison between the different kinds of extreme right websites but I begin with our Italian websites. Which are not difficult to find. All you need to do is use a search engine like Google or Altavista and enter a phrase like 'fascism on the web'. Scrolling down the entries listed on the result pages you will sooner or later find an entry like 'Dux Award' or 'Camerata virtuale' or 'Foedus Italicum' or Siti d'Area (Sites in this area). If you click on the link to Dux Award a page[7] appears where you find this text:

7   Available at http://www.web.tiscali.it/duxaward/ [accessed 28 June 2007 (translator)].

Dux Award Site

The Dux Award is a logo that will be assigned on request to sites which are concerned with the history of fascism and of the Second World War.

The purpose of The Dux Award is to gather together under one logo all the historical and cultural sites which are concerned with the subjects mentioned above in order to facilitate navigation and research.

Every site recommended in this way will be checked by our staff of three people, consisting of a web master, a history expert and a coordinator.

At the end of the check the website will be rated on the basis of the quality of the graphics and content of the site and the link will be added to the page entitled 'Winners'.

The logo that Dux Award assigns to its adherents is clearly visible immediately below this text. It depicts the face of Benito Mussolini flanked by fasces. And as the introductory note says, by visiting the 'Winners' page you can soon find out which sites boast the logo. Right now, as I write[8] they are the following: Il Ventennio Fascista (The two fascist decades),[9] Un Omaggio al Duce (Homage to the Leader – Mussolini),[10] I Documenti della Storia (Historical documents),[11] Fascismo in rete (Fascism on the web),[12] Brigata Nera (Black Brigade),[13] La storia del Duce (Biography of Mussolini),[14] Storia della RSI (History of the Italian Social Republic),[15] Spedizione Punitiva (Punitive Expedition),[16] Sangue Nero (Black Blood),[17] and a few others of the same ilk. The Dux Award site thus forms the centre of a web ring: the listed sites are linked both to the principal site and to each other in a system of interlocking cross-references. And the same is true of Foedus Italicum,[18] Camerata virtuale[19] and Siti d'Area.[20] These sites, like the Dux Award, carry long lists of websites which explicitly refer to the fascist past. But now let's have a look at what these sites are concerned with.

---

8 As of 28 June 2008 [accessed by translator].

9 http://www.piralli.it/ventennio2.htm [accessed 28 June 2007 (translator)].

10 http://on.to/mussolini [accessed 28 June 2007 (translator)].

11 http://www.larchivio.com/storia.htm [accessed 28 June 2007 (translator)].

12 http://www.fascismoinrete.cjb.net/ [accessed 28 June 2007 (translator)].

13 http://it.geocities.com/brigatanera88/ [accessed 28 June 2007 (translator)].

14 http://freeweb.supereva.com/storiadelduce/index.htm?p [accessed 28 June 2007 (translator)].

15 http://digilander.libero.it/trustmatrix/ [accessed 28 June 2007 (translator)].

16 http://www.spedizionepunitiva.tk/ [accessed 28 June 2007 (translator)].

17 http://www.sanguenero.tk/ [accessed 28 June 2007 (translator)].

18 http://digilander.libero.it/fascismoinrete1/foedusitalicum.htm [accessed 28 June 2007 (translator)].

19 http://musagetenero.altervista.org/forum.htm [accessed 28 June 2007 (translator)].

20 http://digilander.libero.it/sitifascisti/ [accessed 28 June 2007 (translator)].

A first distinction can be made immediately. There are three types of extreme right website. In the first category we have those websites that I would define as of a general nature: they are all quite similar and concern fascism, its doctrine, its history and in particular the figure of Benito Mussolini. Websites like La storia del Duce (see above), Il Ras,[21] Fascis Lictoriim,[22] and the already mentioned Brigata, fall into this category. In the second category we have more specialized sites which deal with particular aspects of the history of fascism and Nazism. Sites like Associazione Combattenti Decima Flottiglia Mas,[23] Repubblica Sociale Italiana,[24] and I Leoni Morti[25] fall into this category. Finally, there are some sites that I would define as pure propaganda given that they gather materials of a disparate nature but which are all characterized by and the exaltation of fascism and Nazism, Holocaust denial and a ferocious anti-Semitism. Sites like Kommando Fascista,[26] the 'Fabio Galante' site[27] and Holy War[28] come into this category.

What do you find on this kind of site? Let's begin with those in the first category which are also the most nostalgic. Almost all these sites have the same structure. In fact they usually consist of two sections. The first is devoted to the figure of Mussolini of whom a eulogistic portrait is provided accompanied by photographs of various kinds and supplemented – often – by a selection of his speeches. The second section, on the other hand, is devoted to a revisionist history of the fascist period and sometimes to a denial of the Shoah, the extermination of the Jews in the Nazi concentration camps. The website Il Ras, for example, which is devoted to Mussolini, bears an image of him at the top of the homepage with the logo of the site at its centre and immediately below, this explanatory text:

> The object of this site is to praise Benito Mussolini and fascism because the fascist decades notably changed the history of Italy and also the Italians themselves. For this reason we should eulogize our Duce and thank our grandfathers, forefathers and ancestors who fought for our homeland and who have ensured that fascist ideals have remained rooted in Italian society today. It is now our duty to maintain these ideals and defend them with honour.

---

21 http://ilras.tk/ [accessed 28 June 2007 (translator)].

22 http://www.fascislictorii.too.it/ [accessed 28 June 2007 (translator)].

23 http://www.xflottigliamas.it/ [accessed 28 June 2007 (translator)].

24 http://www.italia-rsi.org/ [accessed 28 June 2007 (translator)].

25 http://www.ileonimorti.it/ [accessed 28 June 2007 (translator)].

26 Last known address http://www.fascismoeliberta.net/kf/MENU.html.

27 Last known address http://crimini.web-gratis.net/. This site frequently changes its web address. For more on this please see p. 79.

28 Last known address http://www.holywar.org/. Another website that comes and goes.

On the left side of the same page there is a menu with these headings: History – Texts and Articles – Philosophy – Multimedia files – Initiatives – Various – Friendly sites – Contacts. In the Texts and Articles sections we find this notification:

> This section is devoted to original historical texts written during the fascist period and to articles which deal with major themes concerning the *ventennio*. This is a very important section for a thorough understanding of the dynamism of the fascist ideal and its physiological traits.
>
> If you want to write some articles for publication on this site send me your work via email and after a careful reading I will see to their publication online. The same applies if you want to send me any original texts in your possession, naturally in accordance with the law on copyright.

Then we find a series of writings by Mussolini and by some other fascist leaders – among which a testimony entitled 'A punitive Florentine expedition' and a selection of chapters from Adolf Hitler's *Mein Kampf*. The Multimedia Files section is curious given that in the Historical Photos section, featuring photos of the Duce and of the fascist period, the words 'All rights reserved. Copyright Einaudi Publisher – Arnoldo Mondadori Publisher' indicate that the photographs were taken from books published by these publishers and presumably written by writers whose democratic credentials are not in doubt. In the Audio Files subsection it is possible to download songs like Faccetta Nera, Tripoli bel suol d'amore, Giovinezza and Stornelli neri. Here too there is something curious – or rather, almost amusing. If you try to download these music files you are taken to a page warning you that 'All these files are password protected. The password is: The Ras will not die'. In this same section it is also possible to download a speech by the Duce entitled 'Win and we will win'. In the Video subsection it is possible to download various videos amongst which official National Fascist Party images of the 'March on Rome'. But let's move on now to the Friendly Sites section. Here too we find a long series of links and referrals to other sites and among these pride of place is assigned to the site Il Duce: Benito Mussolini[29] where 'You can find everything you want and above all you can buy the magnificent perfume *Nostalgia*, the duce's perfume, at an unbeatable price…' The Contacts section is very interesting because the links there take you to other sites and other forms of communication online. For example, if you choose Forum you are taken to a page on the Camerata virtuale website[30] which provides you with access to a forum in which, however, no messages are visible. If, on the other hand, you choose Chat you are again taken to a Camerata virtuale page, this time where you can enter a chat room hosted on the server of irc.azzurra.org.

---

29 Available at http://www.ilduce.net/ [accessed 28 June 2007 (translator)].
30 http://musagetenero.altervista.org/forum.htm.

Let's switch now to Brigata Nera.[31] This site does not differ much from Il Ras. Here we find the same thematic sections and a collection of materials in praise of fascism of a very similar type, if not identical. But this site has an additional section. It's called Revisionism. This section, which you can find, by the way, on many analogous sites, is centrally concerned with Holocaust denial and is based on two communicative strategies. The first consists in recourse to quotations or to the reproduction of entire so-called negationist historical texts. The second consist in displaying photographic documents accompanied by a comment which purports to demonstrate their falsity. Brigata Nera offers a good example. Let's see how this section is constructed. Here is the list of subjects:

AUSCHWITZ: THE FACTS AND THE LEGEND
HOLOCAUST AND REVISIONISM: 33 QUESTIONS AND ANSWERS
THE QUESTIONABLE TRUSTWORTHINESS OF PRIMO LEVI
THE TRUTH ABOUT ANNE FRANK'S DIARY
THE NI-9912 DOCUMENT
THE LEUCHTER REPORT
THE PROBLEM OF THE GAS CHAMBERS
THE HOLOCAUST UNDER THE SCANNER
FALSIFICATIONS ABOUT AUSCHWITZ
NOT GUILTY AT NUREMBERG -1-
NOT GUILTY AT NUREMBERG -2-
NOT GUILTY AT NUREMBERG -3-
THE JEWISH DECLARATION OF WAR AGAINST NAZI GERMANY

I won't go into the particulars of this section now as I'm going to return to them when I analyse another site. I'll limit myself at this point to the observation that most of the material quoted on the site comes from the historian Robert Faurisson. The excerpt below, which appears under the heading, 'Auschwitz: the facts and the legend', comes from one of his books. Faurisson writes that

> At the beginning of 1940, Auschwitz was only a city of 13,000 inhabitants in German Alta Slesia. In May of that year, work was begun in the periphery of Auschwitz, in the area of a Polish artillery barracks, on a transit camp for 10,000 Polish prisoners. In the years that followed, as the war became more onerous, Auschwitz became the centre of a cluster of about forty camps and sub-camps and the capital of an enormous agricultural and industrial complex (mines, petrochemicals, armament factories) where many prisoners, in particular Jews and Poles, worked alongside civilian workers. Auschwitz was, in succession,

---

31 http://it.geocities.com/brigatanera88/home.htm.

a concentration camp, and a forced and free labour camp. It was never an extermination camp (an expression invented by the allies). Despite drastic hygienic measures and numerous hospital buildings and barracks, sometimes equipped with the latest German discoveries in the medical field, typhoid, which was endemic in the Jewish Polish population and among the Russian prisoners of war, caused, together with typhoid fever and other epidemics, devastation in the camps and in the city of Auschwitz among the both concentration camp and civil populations, as well as among the German doctors. And that is why, during the whole existence of the camp, epidemics, united at times with hunger, heat and cold and with terrible working conditions in this swampy zone, caused, between 20 May 1940 and 18 January 1945, the deaths of many people, probably 150,000 prisoners.

The Zio Benito (Uncle Benito) site[32] exhibits analogous characteristics. On the first page we find a foreword in the usual style:

TRUST OBEY FIGHT

THIS WAS THE MOTTO OF THE YOUTH OF LITTORIO
THIS SITE HOLDS A COLLECTION OF DOCUMENTS CONCERNING THE
NATIONAL FASCIST PARTY AND BENITO
MUSSOLINI, A MAN WHO WAS LOVED
AND HATED, WHO WAS ABLE TO INDOCTINATE THE
ITALIANS DURING THE FASCIST DECADES AND TO
CREATE A VERITABLE RELIGION: FASCISM

which is followed immediately by a series of documents of a historical character, for example on the 'black shirts', the 'Muti legion' and the 'Black brigades', Mussolini's testament, a propaganda discourse by Mussolini, the speech delivered by Mussolini – in MP3 format – on the declaration of war, and songs of the time, which as we have seen are available on other sites but here are offered with the a note that 'in making this page we owe particular thanks to Camerata XY of Pavignano (Biella) who has kindly made the CD "Hymns and original songs from the fascist era" available…TO US!'. Nor

---

32 The site has since disappeared. Its last known address was http://www.digilander. libero.it/ZioBenito/index2.htm. It was defaced on 28 January 2005. Website defacement means changing the appearance of a site's home page by substituting another created for the purpose. This operation – or rather this intrusion – requires a high level of skill and technological know-how on the part of the cracker. In the particular case of the Zio Benito home page, it was replaced with another with a red background and a penguin (Linux symbol) in the centre holding a dark red flag. The caption below said: 'Linux … because Penguins have hearts too … with left-wing sympathies … if you really want to enter this fascist site click here'. It was thus still possible to enter the site.

is the ad for Nostalgia Perfume missing: 'Two unisex fragrances, one tough and virile (fresh); the other sweeter and mellower: two perfumes for the two different but complementary sides of the DUCE, a man both severe and reassuring. Two really exceptional fragrances, two perfumes to treasure ...' And to end with, the credo of the true fascist:

<blockquote align="center">
I believe in Italy the immortal
creator of civilization and progress
and in BENITO MUSSOLINI, her great son,
our DUCE loved and unforgotten
who was conceived in the pain and
in the love of the people.
Born of Santa Rosa Maltoni
he suffered under Pietro Badoglio, the new Judas
he was betrayed and imprisoned,
after forty days he was seized and liberated
by way of the highways of the sky.
He returned to Italy to save her honour and
restore her greatness,
but was assassinated and abused.
he sits in the presence of GOD omnipotent father
and is called on by all good Italians
to come and judge the cowards and revenge the dead.
I believe in Universal Fascism,
In the resurrection of Italy,
In the immortality of heroes and martyrs,
In the sacredness of the ideals of the homeland,
In the greatness of her destiny
and in her eternal mission,
So be it.
</blockquote>

The site Fascismo in Rete[33] does not differ in essentials from this formula. Here too we find the usual speeches by the Duce, his biography, his testament and songs of the time which can be downloaded. Only two sections distinguish this site from those above. The first is called 'Flags and Symbols' and apart from different versions of the Italian flag – the national tricolour flag, the tricolour flag of Savoy, the naval tricolour flag and the flag of the Italian Social Republic – it also carries a wide range of Third Reich flags beginning with the swastika. The second section is called 'Neo-fascism' and lists those parties and movements which, according to those responsible for the site, continue to sustain and disseminate the ideals of the fascist period. These

---

33 http://www.fascismoinrete.cjb.net/.

parties and movements are the following: Pino Rauti's Movimento Sociale – Fiamma Tricolore, Forza Nuova, the Fronte Sociale Nazionale and the Movimento Fascismo e Libertà.

I won't take into consideration the other websites that I have listed because at this point the sort of content you find on visiting them should be quite clear. For the most part historical documents concerning Mussolini and the fascist period, which is depicted as a glorious moment in the history of Italy, above all from the point of view of its system of values. Strangely, or at least it seems so to me, no attempt is made to recommend fascism as an improvement on the social system we have today. Nowhere have I read affirmations of the type: trains ran on time then. The communicative strategy of these sites centres on the exaltation of the great man and the great values of which he is the bearer. Mussolini is an undisputed hero, a bit severe perhaps, but always benevolent, generous and altruistic. He did not lead Italy to disaster – on the contrary, he raised Italy to its maximum splendour, reinvigorating her with ideas drawn from Italy's most potent tradition. He did not fall because defeated on that battlefield onto which he hauled millions of Italians but because he was betrayed in cowardly fashion by his own comrades in arms. In short, a knight in shining armour defeated because of human wickedness. What this amounts to is an attempt, flying in the face of all the evidence to the contrary – not so much to uphold a point of view concerning historical events – as rather, by amassing texts removed from any context of reference, to reconstruct history as a story which if not actually a fairy tale, draws its principal narrative archetypes from this literary genre. Mussolini is not the politician who established a dictatorship that lasted two decades but the good hero and warrior who fought and defeated the decline of his country. The fasces are not a symbol of a brutal power that abolished any form of democratic liberty but the wind-blown standard of a small group of courageous men who, like the knights of the Round Table, followed King Arthur through thick and thin. Those who opposed them have neither a face nor an identity and are rarely mentioned. And just as grandfathers of old told their grandchildren the same fairy tale with tiny variations, so these sites narrate a story which is always the same in its constituent elements, adding or subtracting only some details of secondary importance. In this sense, they could seem not only nostalgic but above all conservative in that they seek to recover from the dust of time the memory of one of the darkest moments in Italian history. This is an impression that is reinforced by the fact that they are also very static. Once constructed, and as soon as their authors consider that they have filled them with all the material that is sufficient for the achievement of the objective that they have set themselves, they are in fact often abandoned and rarely updated. Some even seem to date from the late '90s, as is suggested by a page layout which is characteristic of those years, coupled with crude graphics that have been obtained free of charge on the web, like the animated clips and effects created with java applets that were in vogue many years ago. However they are on the net and that is where they remain.

The same is also true, for that matter, of more specialized sites. Take, for example, the veteran association site Decima Mas.[34] It has all the appearance of a small and dusty online museum. As usual the first page contains a slogan, prominently displayed, this time by Junio Valerio Borghese, commander of the X Mas:

> To work men, with spirit and faith. Our little difficulties will all be overcome providing we keep our heads and we remember that because of our order and discipline we soldiers have been entrusted with the job of national reconstruction. Onwards Decima!

Immediately below there is a menu which refers us to the history of this military formation, to an archive of documents, to the divisions of which it was composed, to a list of veteran reunions, and to a page where it is possible to download photos and hymns. There are no historical references apart from those of a military nature concerning the unit. Even fascism goes unmentioned and the Salò Republic is only referred to in passing. The more that I looked at the site the more it reminded me of those books of local history, written by amateur but enthusiastic historians, which contain painstaking accounts of actions of war in which every detail is recorded. And the same thing came to mind when I browsed the site devoted to the veterans of the Salò Republic which has a very similar structure even though the contents are different.[35] But then I thought of the naziskins whom I had got to know and of something that was relatively predictable in a group of the kind, namely that none of them had much of a grounding in extreme right culture or knew any of its most important texts. They had all confessed that they didn't read much, at most a book or two by Stephen King or Tolkien. For them history was limited to the fascist period, about which, moreover, they knew almost nothing. Nor did they have a clearly thought out project of social or revolutionary transformation as a basis for action. All they had was their ferocious entrenchment in a situation of self-isolation in which what counted most was the fact that those with whom they shared this all embracing experience were more than friends because they had become 'camerati', while everyone else formed part of an indistinct mass of enemies, either in actual fact – black people, immigrants, Jews, traitors of the institutionalized right – or potentially –

---

34 This site use to be available at http://www.decimamas.org/index.html but when you enter this address you are redirected to http://www.xflottigliamas.it/ [accessed 28 June 2007 (translator)].

35 http://www.italia-rsi.org/.

ordinary people who persisted in not understanding their 'good' reasons. Hence a distancing of themselves from the world, from people and real problems and a flight into an abstract idea of 'national community' and into a past/present magically reinterpreted in order to extrapolate certain elements that permitted them to find a means of anchoring their everyday routine. To use one of their expressions, their objective was a 'return to Camelot'. In short, nationalism, xenophobia, racism, anti-Semitism, the whole arsenal of intolerance and resentment, were perceived by the naziskins as a cognitive resource which legitimated political action and justified recourse to violence while also functioning as a powerful reducing agent for the complexity of things which enabled those who subscribed to them to find a common ground of identity, albeit an identity founded more on the myth of an imaginary past time than on the inevitable contradictions and tensions of the present.

In consequence sites like those on the X Mas and on the Salò Republic started to appear less dusty to me than they had seemed initially. The cobwebs deposited by time on their contents melted away, and it seemed to me that I could understand what their real message was. The whole operation of recalling what had happened in the war, the actions of this or that seaman, of this or that soldier from Monterosa, functions, in reality – or at least, so it seems to me – as a way of strengthening a sense of identity and as a call to action that has no need of more elaborate ideological trimmings – or for that matter of a sophisticated layout. I would challenge anyone to read the whole of an article like 'Harbingers of glorious days' on the screen of a computer. It is impossible. It is too long, the characters are too small, the details too numerous to remember. It took me almost half an hour to read it all and when I had finished my eyes were burning because of the effort required to focus on that long account written in black on a dark background. You can imagine what would happen if a seventy-year old or a young neo-fascist tried reading it. But the value of this document changes as soon as you stop considering it a simple historical testimony and you consider it as a source of identity and an incitement to action, and as a confirmation of the continuing existence, in the new century, of a social fabric, however limited and isolated, to which it refers. It is not important whether it is read but that it exists.

But there is another aspect that should be noted. The materials on these sites are also found in articles which circulate in print form in far-right environments. For example, in magazines like *L'uomo libero* or *Avanguardia*, or in books produced by publishing companies like *Edizioni Ar*, *Settimo Sigillo* and *All'Insegna del Veltro*. Such publications are quite widely diffused in extreme right milieux, and above all are convenient and easy to obtain. There is no need to possess a computer or to have a connection to the Internet. Just go to a bookshop that specializes in such things or take out a subscription. So what is the need of putting materials on the web too?

That there is such a need, and that the culture of the extreme right is not only transmitted orally in face to face meetings or by means of old media like print, but now has solid roots in the most modern of communication technologies, seems to me further confirmation of how the Internet has become immanent in everyday life, as Barry Wellman puts it, taking on the form of a canvas on which every group can weave its collection of messages, side by side with the innumerable designs that other groups fabricate in order to transmit their messages to their audiences. And it makes little difference on the Internet whether these messages serve to publicize material goods like the latest model of a car or immaterial goods like a kit for the creation of a sense of identity that consists of symbols, icons, norms and values. What does matter is that every section of the canvas is woven in such a way as to create a cognitive experience that is well structured and complete, in which all the components of the symbolic universe that you want to represent are integrated. For this reason I don't find it at all strange that apart from the sites listed up to now you can also find some specializing in memorabilia of the fascist and Nazi epochs, a retro version of the e-commerce that is so much talked about. Many people argue that e-commerce does not work. Apart from some exceptions like e-Bay or Amazon, selling goods online does not seem to produce the astonishing profits long-forecasted by those prophets of the net economy who claimed that e-commerce was a panacea for our stagnant economies, within easy reach, and that all that greengrocers, shoemakers or sellers of peppery cheese needed to do to boost their earnings was seize the opportunity it offered. Not to mention the dotcom sites which sprouted like mushrooms all over the globe. The prophecy was not fulfilled. And it was not fulfilled because people lacked faith, or more simply because they prefer to touch the jar of jam that they wanted to buy. Those who did make it and who survived – apart from the porn sites which did make big profits – were those who created a niche for themselves in a particular goods sector or who coupled online selling with normal selling within the four walls of a shop. That is exactly what two Italian commercial concerns which sell 'marvelous gadgets and souvenirs from the fascist and Third Reich' online seem to be doing. These two virtual shops are called Militaria Souvenir[36] and Militaria Collection.[37] You can find anything and everything in these two shops and it is worthwhile taking a look at the shelves of these two sellers who have a head office, an address, a storeroom, opening hours, a bank account, a name and a surname. Let's begin with Militaria Souvenir where it is possible to find everything that is necessary for reinvigorating tired memories or polishing tarnished ideals. Here is a selection of the merchandise on offer: 1) a set of four clubs with the inscriptions Dux Mussolini, Boia che Molla, Molti

---

36 Available at http://www.militariasouvenir.com/ [accessed 28 June 2007 (translator)].

37 Available at http://www.militariacollection.com/ [accessed 28 June 2007 (translator)].

Nemici Molto Onore, Me ne Frego.[38] The blurb says: This collection of four models is offered at a special launch price of 35 Euros instead of at 40 Euros. Every model carries the inscription Dux Mussolini on one side while the motto on the other differs according to model. 2) Black T-shirts with a choice of three versions: with the flag of the Third Reich, with the symbol of the SS, or classic with swastika. 3) Zippo lighters in two versions: with swastika or with Mussolini's portrait. 4) Watch with image of Hitler impressed on the case 5) Goring and Himmler partly stuffed dolls in reduced scale 6) A Ken type version of Adolf Hitler in a transparent box with changes of uniform.[39] And, of course, a profusion of Third Reich badges, coats of arms and flags.

The Militaria Collection site, on the other hand, does not merely sell memorabilia for nostalgic souls. Here you can buy things other than poorly finished stuffed dolls of Adolf Hitler and models of the Mercedes in which the Führer paraded Unter den Linden. Their catalogue contains a veritable arsenal of guns, pistols, swords and knives. Reproductions, we are warned by the seller, and this is probably true in the case of the guns and pistols, but it is difficult to believe that the same applies to the daggers and swords which, at least on the computer screen, don't seem to be made of tin. 'Manufactured entirely in metal, down to the smallest details. Every pistol has realistic dimensions and weight', says the blurb.[40] And the business cannot be doing badly if, as we are informed, 'Militaria Collection celebrates with all its clients 10 years of activity [...] We began our commercial activity timidly, and not without encountering problems, with only two or three items in our catalogue ... and today we operate through three websites'. Three websites. No, business is going decidedly well.

3. Three singular websites

Now we come to three sites that I have left out of my analysis up to now and which I class as pure propaganda. If I treat them as a case apart this is because, unlike those above, rather than address a selected audience composed of the already convinced they go decidedly beyond such limits. They do not exist to confirm an identity or a commitment to militant action. Instead their objective is to liberally spread an entire repertoire of racism, xenophobia,

---

38 Fascist slogans. 'Dux Mussolini' can be translated as 'Mussolini our leader'; 'Boia che Molla' as 'Whoever gives up the struggle is a traitor (literally an executioner)'; 'Molti Nemici Molto Onore' as 'Many enemies much honour' and the meaning of 'Me ne Frego' is 'Who gives a damn'.

39 Ken is a male doll in the Barbie series. In truth paradoxically this Adolf Hitler doll looks just like Charlie Chaplin in *The Great Dictator* (1940).

40 Available at http://www.armscollection.com/pugnali.htm [accessed 28 June 2007 (translator)].

anti-Semitism and religious traditionalism in an openly eulogistic fashion. The first of these sites is called Kommando Fascista.[41] From a graphical point of view it is rather well constructed. All the pages have a black background and the images are clear and sharp. It is easy to navigate. The material is very varied. It is divided into thematic sections of which the most important are those devoted to fascism and Nazism, easily identifiable thanks to the presence of two eye-catching logos – on the left an eagle with spread wings above fasces, on the right another above a swastika – and that devoted to the Holocaust. In addition there is section for the download of files. The first impression you get on browsing its pages is that here is a site that is far from static and that has a fairly high number of visitors. It appears to be updated frequently and it offers much more in the way of interactivity than nostalgic websites. I forgo offering a description of the pages dedicated to fascism and Nazism since apart from images of the two dictators in various poses they only contain historical material – which it is possible to print thanks to a function designed for the purpose – that is pretty similar to that seen in the sites above, though an integral version of *Mein Kampf* does stand out. I prefer to concentrate on three sections alone. The first is entitled 'Revisionism'.

> What is Revisionism? It is an attempt to understand something about those intrigues with which World War II ended, when the winners claimed the right not only to impose their will on the defeated but to arbitrarily distribute right and wrong with the objective of staking a definitive claim on the future. We must now re-appropriate that future by establishing once and for all the historical truth.

This declaration leads into the many pages devoted to the denial of the Shoah. I will try to convey an idea of how this subject is treated by simply quoting some of the theme headings and their accompanying blurb.

THE TRUTH ON ANNE FRANK'S DIARY
Anne Frank's diary: a sensational fraud!
GUIDE TO A CRITICAL READING OF ANNE FRANK'S DIARY

QUESTIONS AND ANSWERS ON THE HOLOCAUST
What proof have we that the Nazis practiced genocide or that they deliberately exterminated 6 million Jews?

None. The only proof is the testimony of individual "survivors". These depositions are extremely contradictory and no 'survivor' claims to have been a witness to the gassing. There is no concrete proof of any kind: no piles of ashes, no cremation ovens capable of doing the work required, no piles of clothes, no soap made with human fat, no lamp shades made of human skin, no precise dates, no demographic statistics.

---

41 This site, which is no longer available, used to have two addresses: http://www. fascismeliberta.net/kf/MENU.html and http://kommandofascista.88.to (translator's note).

THE JEWISH DECLARATION OF WAR ON NATIONAL SOCIALIST GERMANY

Long before the Hitler government began to limit the rights of the Jews, the leaders of the world-wide community of Jews declared war on the "new Germany", that is to say, at a time when the American government, and even Jewish leaders in Germany, were advising against being precipitate with regards to relations with Hitler's regime.

The war waged by international Jewish leaders against Germany not only caused the institution of anti-Jewish measures but also laid the foundations for a sort of economic-political understanding between Hitler's regime and the leaders of the Zionist movement who hoped that tensions between Germans and Jews would lead to a massive exodus of Jews towards Palestine. In short, there was a tactical alliance between the Nazis and the founders of the modern State of Israel, a circumstance that many would like to see forgotten today. Up till now it has always been believed (erroneously) that as soon as Hitler was elected Leader and Chancellor his government immediately began a policy of repression towards German Jews, closing them in concentration camps and beginning violent actions of terror and retaliation against them. If on the one hand there were isolated acts of violence against Jews in Germany after Hitler came to power, on the other they were not officially encouraged or tolerated.

ARE THESE PHOTOGRAPHS PROOF OF THE NAZI EXTERMINATION OF JEWS?

In all the photographs reproduced both the people depicted and the person who took the photograph are unknown. This is a prerogative that is characteristic of almost all the so-called "photographic proof" concerning the assassination of Jews.

These extracts, in their brevity and dryness, cannot provide an adequate account of what is written in long pages. I refer my readers to the sections 'Scanning the Holocaust'[42] and 'Why are these things not taught in school'[43] for the illuminating experience of reading them for themselves and move on to the Download section, where it is possible to download texts of this tenor:

If Hitler had written a novel, what would it have been like? Like this: THE LORD OF THE SWASTIKA

---

42 Which used to be available at http://www.fascismoeliberta.net/kf/OALLOSCANNER. htm (translator's note).

43 Which used to be available at http://www.fascismoeliberta.net/kf/SCUOLA.htm (translator's note).

Texts for political education courses: FASCIST CULTURE

THE HOLOCAUST INDUSTRY. This offers an analysis and an indictment of the Holocaust industry.

Here is the truth about the Jewish race! PROTOCOLS OF THE WISE MEN OF ZION

And there is also this game:

GHETTO BLASTER: AN APPEALING NATIONAL SOCIALIST GAME. THE TARGETS TO DESTROY ARE JEWS, GYPSIES, BLACKS ETC. BONUS POINTS ARE REPRESENTED BY SWASTIKAS WHICH ARE ALWAYS WELCOME AND WHEN THEY ARE EARNED A FANTASTIC SIEGH HEIL OF TIMES GONE BY IS TRIGGERED!

I've tried this game. It is really nasty. It consists in using three baseball balls with swastikas imprinted on them to hit the grotesquely represented faces of Jews, Gypsies, Blacks and other victims of prejudice. In short it amounts to a very crude neo-Nazi version of BreakOut, a well-known game for PCs.

Lastly, I will try to summarize, by using short excerpts, what the section called 'Opinion polls' contains. The most significant polls seem to be those which I can see right now as I write. The first poses this question: 'Contemporary society, at world level, is afflicted with many cancers. Which do you think should be the first to be eliminated?' I was not surprised to see that the most popular choices were Semitism and/or Zionism, partitocracy, and dictatorial regimes based on mass media manipulation. But the second poll is even more explicit: 'From Slovenia to the Baltic, neo-Nazi movements have shown that they are a political force to be reckoned with. What is your opinion?' The possible answers are naturally in tune with the question: 'This shows that fortunately there still exists an elite of human beings who think for themselves' and 'It is too soon to celebrate, it is necessary to reinforce international contacts'.

The second site which I propose to examine owes its name to its creator: a certain Fabio Galante.[44] I use his name because it appears in the title of his website and so I am not revealing anything secret or breaking the rule which demands that the names of the people of whom you talk be changed. This site is slightly different from that above in that it is constructed around

---

44 Fabbio Galante's site has no fixed abode. When visited by Antonio Roversi it was available at http://crimini.web-gratis.net/enter.htm. At some date it moved to http://www. komunismo.clara.co.uk/ but on attempting to visit this site I found that the server hosting the site had closed it down and posted the notice 'THIS WEBSPACE HAS BEEN SUSPENDED FOR ABUSE Please contact- Tel- 0845 234 0712. Email- support@clara.net Clara.net Abuse Team' [accessed 28 June 2007 (translator)].

three thematic sections: Eulogies of Nazism, Holocaust denial and the denunciation of the crimes committed by past communist regimes. In order to give you a quick impression of Sig. Fabio Galante's neo-Nazi site I quote the alert message that appears whenever you visit a page.

> Attention. This site is monitored by the *Centro Informatico per la Ricerca sui Crimini Telematici* (C.I.R.C.T) [Centre for Research on Criminal use of Information Technology – translator]. The TCP/IP number from which you have come has been automatically registered and decodified and a remote system controlled by the Israeli secret service has discovered your name, which has been instantly inserted into a database of potential neo-Nazis. A Postal Police Officer could contact you, from this moment in time onwards, to check on your political choices. Thanks to the Law on Privacy you can be certain that your personal file will never be published on the Internet or by organs of the press, radio or television, except if new measures are taken which make it inevitable. Feeling frightened eh? This time you can breathe a sigh of relief. No one will come to your house and seize you at three in the morning to pillory you, at least for now. Now you can look at this page. The webmaster: Fabio GALANTE.

Apart from the usual eulogistic images of Mussolini and Hitler, the editor devotes a great deal of space to three themes: Holocaust denial, the Nuremberg trials and the crimes of past communist regimes. I think it is worth citing an extract that illustrates the Sig. Galante's Holocaust denial argument.[45]

THE INFAMOUS GERMAN GAS CHAMBERS
(OR RATHER ZYKLON AND THE GERMAN
DISINFESTATION CHAMBERS)

It is estimated that in Germany during the war almost 32 million items of clothing were treated with Zyklon B. This sanitary measure certainly saved hundreds of thousands of people, amongst whom a significant number of Jewish prisoners in concentration camps, from death as a result of typhoid.

Zyklon was consigned in tin containers in the form of discs, tablets or granules. Wood pulp or diatomaceous earth, a brown granular mass, served as support. The gas is liberated on air contact. The duration of the chemical process depends on the air temperature. When the point of sublimation, 25.7°C, is reached, most of the gas is released in half an hour. More time is necessary at lower temperatures.

Let us now look at how Zyklon B was used according to two German documents of the war period.

---

45 This page is still available at http://www.komunismo.clara.co.uk/auschwitz.htm [accessed 28 June 2007 (translator)].

Disinfestation chambers built by DEGESCH (Deutsche Gesellschaft für Schädlingsbekänofung) were widely used for the delousing of clothes. These chambers had a standard volume of 10m³ and were hermeneutically sealed.

The clothes that were to be deloused were hung from battens or put on a trolley.

The disinfestation chambers were heated to a temperature of between 25 and 35°C. The gas that was released from the Zyklon granules was diffused through a ventilation system. The same system was used to air the chamber rapidly using pre-warmed air.

The box of Zyklon opened automatically when the ventilation system was set in operation and its contents were poured into a recipient; this was done to avoid the possibility that granules ended up forgotten on the ground when the chambers were cleaned because they could liberate gas for hours and injure human beings.

The gas treatment lasted at least an hour, aeration 15 minutes. Then the deloused clothes were brought out into the open air. The chambers were prepared by expert staff (see F.Puntigam/H.Breymesser/E.Bernfus, Blausäuregaskammern zur Fleckfieberabewehr [literally: Gas chambers utilizing hydrocyanic acid in the fight against petechial typhoid], a Reichsarbeitsblatt special publication, Berlino 1943).

Obviously, the disinfestation of places which could not be heated or sealed and which lacked ventilation systems, like homes, boats etc, had to be done using other methods. A document setting out regulations concerning the utilization of the gas published in 1942 by the sanitary service of the Protettorato di Boemia-Moravia with the title Richtlinien für die Anwendung von Blausäure (Zyklon) zur Ungeziefervertilgung [Regulations for the use of cyanide (Zyklon) for the destruction of parasites] describes how the treatment should be carried out in a building. According to this text, disinfestation should be undertaken by a team of at least two men trained for this work. All disinfestation specialists were equipped with a gasmask with two special filters for hydrocyanic acid, a detector of residual gas, a syringe with antidote and written authorization. Before beginning the operation a special notice depicting a skull and drawn up in several languages had to be affixed to the door of the building. A guard kept unauthorized people at a distance. According to the same text, the most dangerous part of the operation was aeration which had to last not less than 20 hours.

These operating instructions were presented at Nuremberg as a document for the prosecution under the heading N1-9912, but no attentive observer would have failed to notice that the indications which it gave on the characteristics of Zyklon clearly contradicted those who asserted that it had been used for the gassing in mass of human beings.

WHAT IS AT STAKE

Without the German reparations which began to arrive in the course of the first ten years of its existence, the State of Israel would not have half of its present infrastructure: all the trains in Israel are German, the ships are German, as is its electricity and a great part of its industry [...] not to mention the pensions paid to the survivors.

I frankly admit that, though I am aware that it is dangerous, I find it difficult to take Sig. Fabio Galante and his site seriously. The alert message cited above seems to me, in itself, an indication of a disturbed mind. And this impression is confirmed for me every time I read the section devoted to communist crimes. How can you take someone seriously who writes something like this?

CANNIBALISM AND COMMUNISM[46]

For a long time now strange stories have been circulating about the presumed alimentary habits of Russians. That which is best known is the classic story-legend of communist "baby-eaters"... but is it true?

Or is this something that happens sporadically and which has been exaggerated?

I have collected some documents concerning episodes of cannibalism in the ex Soviet Union and about the probable causes that have contributed to the growth of this legend.

4. How to deny without ignoring

At this point I propose to pause a moment. I will take advantage of the break to formulate a schematic summary of the rhetorical practices that we have seen in operation on the sites that have been listed up to now. For this purpose, I'm going to appropriate, with various modifications and many adjustments, some things said by Valentina Pisanty in her book on historical revisionism[47] which I find are also applicable to this communicative context. My schema could be summarized in a slogan: who denies does not ignore. And, precisely because they know, they try to reconcile cognitive dissonances between what they know and what they are prepared to admit by resorting to a series of easily identifiable stratagems. These stratagems, or better, these clichés are:

---

46 This page is still available at http://www.komunismo.clara.co.uk/orrifi.htm accessed 28 June 2007 (translator)].

47 Pisanty, V. (1998, *L'irritante questione delle camere a gas: logica del negazionismo* (Milano: Bompiani).

1. Narrative fragmentation. This consists in focusing attention on some particular aspects as if they exist in a temporal vacuum. The course of events is broken into lots of little fragments so as to lose any sense of temporal continuity and weaken the emotional impact. This stratagem is based on a perception that is also common to other social milieux and which sociologists call 'the telescope effect'. What happened to us in the moment n is remembered as happening in the moment n -t.

2. Historical decontextualisation. Or rather, presenting events as if they are unconnected with one another. An example of this is the exaltation of X Mas as a purely military formation while forgetting the historical context of reference, namely the Salò Republic and more generally the situation of civil war that Italy was experiencing in that period.

3. De-dramatization of symbols. This is achieved by misrepresenting or inverting the significance of an event or a fact in order to weaken its value. This has been seen in the case of the gas chambers: they are represented as places of disinfestation and not as instruments of death for millions of innocent people.

4. Semantic shift. Valentina Pisanty has written many illuminating pages on this to which I refer you which show the communicative tricks which are most frequently used by propagandists of the Holocaust denial mould. This strategy is all about searching for a different 'meaning' with which to name a certain event. For example, 'transfer' is used instead of 'deportation'; you don't say 'extermination' but 'final solution' and so on. In this way language becomes an instrument for the dispersal or hiding of meanings.

5. Documentary totemism. This strategy is based on looking for things which are mistaken or misleading in this or that document. Those of you who have time to read the various confutations of Anne Frank's Diary will be able to see this strategy in operation for yourselves. The various arguments used for raising doubts about photographic documents showing the life of deportees in concentration camps and about the very existence of the concentration camps themselves can be viewed in these same terms.

6. Thematic suppression. Or rather 'taking history away from the winners'. All the sites I have listed are characterized by a perspective which re-evaluates the fascist and Nazi period. But since it is not possible for them to make a direct defence of fascism or Nazism without bringing up things that are heinous, they resort to distortions which, on the one hand, are silent on what has been historically established, and which, on the other, serve to cast the winners as victimizers. In short, if fascism and Nazism do not have a good reputation that is to be attributed to the fact that their story was written by the winners, or worse, by the artificers of a Jewish Masonic plot who had every interest in denigrating a period and a social system which were unique in terms of their 'modernity' and 'anti-conformism'.

5. Holy War and the Jewish mafia

Having made these clarifications we can now continue with our journey on the Internet. The last Italian site that I propose to visit is called Holy War and I don't think that there are words that can describe it. Or at least, I find it hard to find them. I have examined it carefully and one section made me smile: that in which it claimed that Nazism is the product of a Jewish plot. It is an argument that is so implausible that the idea that it seriously occurred to someone makes me think that the human imagination knows no limits and that in comparison science fiction writers are amateurs.[48] Then I stopped laughing. Initially I thought that the only thing I could do was let the images speak for themselves and describe them without comment. But then I changed my mind. A synthesis of the images alone would not do justice to this site. So, first of all, I shall give you the address: http://www.holywar. org.[49] And secondly, I will give it the introduction it deserves. So that what it contains is clear beyond any doubt.

The Holy War website is very rich in sections, all of which have been constructed around one unique theme: a ferocious anti-Semitism that oozes from every page, from every phrase, from every image and from every word. From this point of view, I believe that it has few equals on earth (only some American sites – as I shall show – reach these levels of ruthlessness). It expresses its anti-Semitic arguments through 1) An explicit defence of Nazism which stands in contrast to the argument that Nazism is the product of a Judaic Zionist ideology (emblematically summed up in the affirmation that 'Hitler's surname is Jewish'). However, this defence of Nazism is used purely as an instrument for expressing Holocaust denial arguments. 2) A virulent attack on the Catholic Church, accused of having betrayed its apostolic mission by having fallen prey to the Jewish mafia. 3) A disgusting – because of the way in which it is conducted through a collection of horrific photographs – campaign against abortion. 4) Above all – an explicit exhibition of anti-Semitism that not only accuses Jews of having committed every possible crime from the Big Bang onwards but goes as far as to provide a long list of the surnames of all Italian Jewish families. 5) Finally – and how could it be missed out? – an accusation of responsibility for crimes perpetrated by communist regimes. But let's take them in order, analysing a section at a time.

The first section that I'm going to consider is that devoted to the Catholic Church. This is the lightest section and I can introduce it by summarizing the

---

48 In reality this is an interpretation which has enjoyed a certain popularity in some areas of the far-right and goes back to, among others, Julius Evola. On this see Galli, G. (1989), *Hitler e il nazismo magico* (Milano: 1989).

49 This is the last known address (translator's note).

content of a number of webpages which are emblematic of the convictions of those who run the site – namely, that it is necessary to return to a traditionalist conception of the faith and to abolish the reforms introduced by the Second Vatican Council and that Judaism has managed to worm its way into the Church insinuating itself into the pontificate of John Paul II and seducing many other leading figures. Indeed it is repeatedly insisted upon that 'Wojtyla is an anti-Catholic pope' and to this end he is shown kissing the Qur'an or meeting with rabbis from the Jewish Community. His declarations are laboriously sifted through to demonstrate that he was a heresiarch. The Second Vatican Council, of which John Paul II is said to have been a defender, is called 'modernist dung'. All this because 'the most perverse of conspiracies against the Holy Church is about to be consummated. Her enemies are plotting to destroy her most sacred traditions by realizing reforms which are as audacious and malevolent as those of Calvin, Zwingli and other heresiarchs, all in the name of the fiction of modernizing the Church and bringing her up to date but with the hidden agenda of opening the door to communism, accelerating the destruction of the free world and preparing for the future destruction of Christianity'. According to this conspiratorial vision, with which all the pages devoted to modern Catholicism are impregnated, a single project brings together a diverse group of plotters – Americans, Israelis, Protestants, rockers, homosexuals and even Nazis – and what unites them is one undisputable fact, that they are Jews. Marx – 'whose real name was Kissel Mordekay' – was a Jew. President Bush is a Jew. Some Cardinals, among them Cardinal Bea – were or are Jews. Even 'Adolf Frankenberger Schicklengruber Hitler was the nephew of the Jew Frankenberger, whose origins were Jewish Hungarian'. And so to the climax of this delirium: 'Adolf Eichmann was Jewish. Born in Haifa, he talked Yiddish'. All these people – dead, living, and to come – have formed, according to the authors of Holy War, a 'Judaical mafia'. They want to destroy the Catholic Church, undermine the foundations of the Western world, annihilate its customs and extinguish any form of free thought.[50]

Here then is the first point: a 'Judaical mafia' is at work which has clear aims. And if these objectives are malevolent and perverse it is because its components are Nazis. I confess that I experienced a certain difficulty in understanding this equation: Jews = Nazis, but convinced that every form of madness has its own logic and having patiently browsed many pages of Holy War I reconstructed that logic in the following terms. Judaism and Nazism, according to the authors of the site, have a minimum common denominator and this common denominator is called Zionism.[51] Jews, all Jews are Zionists, they argue, but the Nazis were also Zionist; their plans did not involve the

---

50 Op. cit. See the section 'The Anti-Church plan to dominate the world'.
51 Op. cit. See the section 'Zionism and National Socialism'.

destruction of the Jews, nor was there any Holocaust. They only exercised a certain amount of pressure on the people of the diaspora in order to encourage them to return to Palestine and found their own state. And here we come to the chapter concerning the negation of the Shoah. The object of this denial is not so much to cleanse Nazism of its criminal history as to establish that Jews are falsifiers. Put in simple terms, the idea that the authors of the site want to offer the visitor is that Nazism was the product of a Judaical ideology and that Nazism served as a docile instrument for the construction of the image of the Jew as a victim. But for what reason was this machination orchestrated? Simple: it was constructed by the Jews themselves in order to clean up their image – to remove that association with absolute evil which derived from being guilty of the greatest crime in history: deicide. Because this is what the Jews were charged with: with being deicides, and this crime is so rooted in their nature that for century after century, for generation after generation it has made them the most despicable of all humanity. And the task that Holy War has taken on itself is that of revealing the many faces with which these despicable beings act on the face of the earth. One of these faces – amongst the many – is that they are intrinsically liars. Mendacious to the point of presenting themselves as the victims of a machination that they had created themselves, while the real victims were the German people. There are various sections on the site where these two levels are intertwined: 'Judaism unmasked', 'The parabola of the perfidious Jews', 'Jews reviewed', 'The Jewish homicide ritual', 'St. John Chrysostom's sermon against the Jews', 'St. Augustine's treatise against the Jews' and, naturally, 'Protocols of the Learned Elders of Zion'(in an integral version). But it is most obvious in the section 'Photographic falsification for propaganda purposes and the Jewish Holocaust'.[52] Here all those techniques of symbolic de-dramatization utilized on other sites are taken up once again and refined. The visitor is deluged with shocking images which are commented on in captions whose pseudo-scientific tones and whose references to unknown historians are designed to demonstrate how the Holocaust never happened and that, on the contrary it was a post-war invention, constructed by the 'Judaical mafia' in order to overturn the stereotype of the Jew as a deicide, and hence as an executioner, which had accompanied the Jews for centuries and transform it into that of the Jew as a victim.

I will return in a moment to this point because there is no limit to ignominy and the Holy War site shows how it is possible to choose the road of hate and intolerance in total tranquility of spirit. First, though, I want to note some inconsistencies. Or at least things that appear that way to the reader, given that tolerance of incoherence and of incompatibility is characteristic

---

52 Op. cit. In the 'Jewish falsification' subsection of 'Historical revisionism'.

of sectarianism. I have already described how the Holy War site is totally pervaded by the idea of a Zionist conspiracy that colours and influences all and how this conspiracy is guided by a 'Judaical mafia' with many tentacles – since apart from Jews there are also Protestants, rockers and homosexuals among its members. To these must be added Muslims, to whom the section 'Get to know Islam' is dedicated. I admit that reading this section was quite instructive given that it contained some historical information that I did not know and in the end I found a judgement that was less drastic than that on Judaism. In fact we are told that 'faced with his brothers who have been led astray by Islam, the Christian can do much better than try to penetrate, in a way that is almost sacrilegious, the mystery of divine mercy, in spite of the firm and unambiguous teachings we have just considered. In reality the Christian must take upon himself a double duty: that of praying for the conversion of Muslims and that of working to ensure that this conversion becomes possible'. This seems like an invitation to tolerance. But this invitation is in total contradiction with the declaration that appears on the homepage: 'No to Turkey in Europe' (which refers to the possibility that Turkey might enter the European Community) for the simple reason that the entrance of a Muslim country might cause the de-Christianization of Catholic countries. But it is also in contraction of the criticism levelled at Pope John Paul II for having kissed the Qur'an and having affirmed that 'Muslims worship a real God' and that 'the plan of salvation will also include Muslims'. To these assertions, in fact, the authors of Holy War reply: 'Only Catholics can worship God' and 'It is pure heresy to say Salvation is for Muslims'. But this position contradicts the campaign of support for armed Islamic groups in Iraq and Palestine which is found in many other sections and which is coherent with the anti-Jewish position of the site. In short, against Muslims on a religious level, supporters on a political level.[53]

And now I come to the two sections which are the most repugnant. The first is called 'Abortion. The only holocaust in history'. I limit myself to indicating its presence because I confess that I have only visited it once and I have no intention of doing so again. Let's be clear about this: everyone is free to think what they want and follow their own conscience with regard to this issue. The pro-abortion and anti-abortion positions have equal dignity if expressed with rational arguments and, above all, if they are expressed calmly. Holy War, on the other hand, sustains its anti-abortion argument by going for a devastating emotional impact: it displays a series of images which would make Jack the Ripper throw up. Photographs of foetuses in bottles, or in the grip of surgeon's pincers, follow one another and make you

---

53 These mental acrobatics stretch even to publishing several Vauro cartoons which appeared in *Il Manifesto* (the left-wing Italian newspaper) attacking Bush and the behaviour of the coalition army in Iraq and Afghanistan.

think that only a Doctor Mengele would have the insensitivity to collect and choose this kind of material. The second section, the richest of the whole site, is that in which – through the use of cartoons – we are supplied with caricatures of Jews showing all the evil things of which they are held to be guilty. It is called 'Cartoons! To make you laugh and make you think!' Here every cartoon draws on the predictable clichés of anti-Semitic iconography. In some cases Jews are represented as small with hooked noses and beards; in others as fat and greasy with money falling out of their pockets. There is the Jew who insults Jesus at the foot of the cross and the Jew that picks up children with sweets. In one cartoon a Jew draws a swastika on a wall of the synagogue and the caption reads 'Hey Rabbi, what are you doing? Stop this racist Jewish provocation'. In another cartoon you can see an obese smug Jew sitting on a globe with the caption 'Money is the god of the Jews. In order to satisfy their avidity they have committed the greatest of crimes'. And so on for page after page. But, since ignominy, as has been said, has no limits, this site also offers a list, in alphabetical order of the surnames – 9,800 are specified – of all the Jewish families in Italy, perhaps in case someone wants to act on the call to arms implicit in the images which I have described.[54] This section is scrupulously organized by category. I quote: '1) Surnames which are geographically Italian, 2) German surnames from the four German communities and from around Italy, particularly from Milan, 3) Spanish surnames from Livorno and especially from Tuscany, 4) Oriental surnames, particularly from Milan and Naples, 5) Jewish surnames from various parts of Italy, particularly from Tuscany, 6) Greek surnames from Trieste 7) Surnames by profession 8) Catholic surnames, the result of mixed marriages with a Jewish girl. These will have to be studied separately by someone who is in a position to make a count of Catholic surnames, 9) surnames of diverse origins'. After this clarification the compiler adds 'And here without more to do is the list of the surnames'. A: Aadith, Abadì, Abeles, Abenaim, Abeniacar, Abib, Abigdor, Aboaf, Abramson, Abravanel, Abulaff and so on …

And with this macabre list I end my review of the Italian sites. I hope that I have represented them accurately. I don't want to draw conclusions which claim to be definitive. At this point everyone can come to their own conclusions, perhaps visiting the sites I have mentioned in person. But having spent many hours browsing their pages I cannot get a question out of my head: is this the price we have to pay for an Internet that is free? A question which is all the more painful – painful because I believe strongly in the goodness and beauty of this instrument of communication – given the presence of sites which are far worse than Kommando Fascista, Razza Ariana or Holy War

---

54 Op. cit., in 'Jewish surnames', a subsection of 'Judaism unmasked'.

in terms of anti-Semitism, intolerance, racial hatred, Nazi apologetics or celebration, Holocaust denial and incitement to violence.[55]

6. Neo-Nazi American sites

In order to find them you can use – apart from the Simon Wiesenthal Centre annual report that has already been mentioned – a webpage which neatly lists many of them. It is called Micetrap Top 88 sites[56] and it is a mine of information. Thanks to it you can discover, for example, the existence of the First United Church of Adolf Hitler and of its website,[57] or that at a shop called Worse than Hell[58] you can buy T-shirts – customized in style and colour – with the slogans like 'Kill black babies before they become criminals', 'Bring back slavery' or 'Love him or hate him, Hitler killed tons of Jews'. But I'm not going to analyse them as I have been doing: there are too many of them and even if I were to select the most significant I doubt that this would be useful. Scrolling the list on Micetrap you soon realize how many of them there are and in how many languages they appear. I think that it is more useful to make some observations concerning the American sites alone – which are certainly the most numerous. And I begin with a premise of a general kind: the American far right is a collection of disparate groups characterized by different and even conflicting ideologies but they have some features in common. These common elements are: strong feelings of hatred towards particular social groups which is manifested in the form of racism or anti-Semitism; an equally strong contempt for the authority of the federal government; close ties with the Ku Klux Klan and with European neo-Nazi organizations (and this is something that should always be borne in mind: the American far right has close relations with both the Ku Klux Klan and with the International Nazi movement); and finally subscription to a religious, almost cosmological vision of the creation of humanity. With regard to this last point, I'll give you a brief example: the White Aryan Resistance (WAR for short) movement which also has its own website.[59] This movement was founded in 1983 by Tom Metzger,[60] a TV repairman who for many years

---

55 I will return to this question in the conclusion.

56 Available at http://www.micetrap.net/top88/. Other useful sources of information are The Hate Directory available at http://www.bcpl.net/~rfrankli/hatedir.htm, and the Anti-Defamation League report *Poisoning the Web: Hatred Online*, available at http://www.adl.org/poisoning_web/introduction.asp. [All these sites were accessed 29 June 2007 (translator)].

57 Last known address http://www.churchofhitler.com/.

58 Available at http://www.tshirthell.com/ [accessed 29 June 2007 (translator)].

59 Available at http://www.resist.com/ [accessed 29 June 2007 (translator)].

60 See http://www.adl.org/learn/ext_us/Metzger.asp for biographical information on Tom Metzger [accessed 29 June 2007 (translator)].

conducted a talk show called *Race and Reason* on a Californian TV channel. The guests on this show often discussed the genetic inferiority of the Jews and other ethnic minorities in America and the menace to the white 'race' represented by mixed race marriages. Many of these discussions centred on skin pigmentation as an element that confirmed white superiority. Whites alone can blush and only those who can have 'blood in the face' are truly human.[61] Other races, blacks and Jews, do not blush and therefore are not human beings. They are sub-human.

I have also said, however, that these movements are not all the same. An example of this is the skinhead movement.[62] As the reader probably knows, the skinhead movement was originally born in Britain in the mid '70s.[63] It was born in the peripheries of the great industrialized cities, where there was a strong working class presence. However, these were years in which Britain was changing and these changes concerned, above all, the economic structure of the country. The hardest hit were the lowest strata of the working class: the least skilled, the worst paid, those whose jobs were physically the most demanding. While restructuring increased demand for skilled workers capable of doing complex jobs, demand for unskilled manual workers fell. It was a process which had two faces. Those who adapted to it, those who were capable of changing with the times, suddenly found the possibility of a better future opening up before them, with greater opportunities for improving both their professional position and their social condition. In technical terms, we can say that these workers became more upwardly mobile and they could hope to achieve a social status that approached that of the lower strata of the middle class. On the other hand, those who did not adapt risked exclusion from the job market and faced the possibility of unemployment, or at best underpaid casual employment. In short: one portion of the working class, the lowest strata, those employed in work of a solely manual nature, the 'rough and tough', began to disappear. These two faces of a social process of wide ranging consequences were reflected in the life styles of those young people who had been born into, and grew up in, the working class. Those who saw the social condition of their parents improve gave birth to the Mod movement, composed of young people whose external appearance – dark well-groomed clothes and matching ties, hair slightly long, polished well-made shoes (The Beatles in some ways, at least initially, mirrored this youth

---

61 Ridgeway, J. (1990), *Blood in the face* (New York. Thunder's Mouth Press).

62 See http://www.hammerskins.net/ [accessed 29 June 2007 (translator)].

63 On the birth of the skinhead movement in England see Brake, M. (1974), 'The Skinheads. An English Working Class Subculture', in *Youth and Society*, **2**; Clarke, J. (1976), 'The Skinheads and the Magical Recovery of Community', in Hall S. and Jefferson T. (eds), *Resistance through Rituals* (London: Hutchinson), and Knight, N. (1982), *Skinhead* (London: Omnibus Press).

culture) – manifested their hopes of improvement. In contrast, those who belonged to working class families 'in decline' gave life to the skinhead movement. They were aware of belonging to a social group on the road to extinction – or at least which was strongly menaced with extinction – and that this process was unstoppable. The world around them was changing: the economy was changing, society was changing, styles of life were changing, and those very values which had sustained the working class until that moment were changing too. (It is worth remembering that Britain has always been a country of strong class divisions with a system of social stratification that was almost impermeable, that made movement from one class to another very difficult, with the result that every social stratum is characterized by its own model of life, its own system of values and even its own model of territorial settlement). Well, faced with this threat of extinction, the skinheads decided to react at least on a symbolic level by adopting a style of dress and an attitude that conserved the memory of a social figure that was disappearing: that of the manual worker who made a living doing a job that was hard, sustained by cultural values that derived from his condition. Hardness, pride in being able to bear physical hardship, standing your ground in violent conflict, strong solidarity with peers (workmates) etc. In short: a style that was masculine and violent. Hence the type of clothing they wore: heavy work boots, plain jeans – and above all, shaved heads. All emblems which hailed back to the figure of the rough tough worker. These first skinheads were – and still are – called 'original', because their existence revolved essentially about their appearance and their shared taste for Oi! music. With time, however, this movement diversified. From that common root sprung two other movements of which I have already spoken. The first are called 'Nazi skinheads' and are composed of young skinheads who have adopted an ideology which is a mixture of nationalism, xenophobia, and nostalgia for a Nazi-fascist past. The second is called 'Sharp' and opposes the first, having taken up diametrically opposed positions. They are connected in many cases – at least in Italy – to the Social Centres for young people dominated by the far left.

The American version of the skinhead movement borrowed many features from the European Nazi skinheads. In particular they have taken up their emphasis on the 'whiteness' of their ethnic roots and their tendency to translate their idea of racial supremacy into violent action. And thus, just as, at the beginning of the '80s, a 'game' called *paki-bashing*, which consisted in small groups of skinheads hunting Pakistanis and beating up anyone they met with olive skins without asking too many questions – and if they were not Pakistani but Indian or Thai or Philippine it didn't matter, they weren't white and that was reason enough to give them a lesson – was popular among English skinheads, so, in the same way, American skinheads took up *nigger-bashing*, hunting 'negroes', an activity that could be defined the result of a cultural contamination between the English 'ambush' and the American practice of 'lynching' that goes back to the Ku Klux Klan. In this case, however, it is necessary to emphasize that this is not a mode of behaviour based, except in a minimal sense, on an anthropological premise. The rhetorical figure that comes into play in the imagination of the American skinhead and which unleashes their racist violence is not in fact that of the biological 'supremacy' of whites so much as that of the 'dangerousness' of ethnic minority groups – the menace they represent to the majority that can 'blush'.

Last of all, I want to mention a radical group that is quite old and which goes by the name of Posse Comitatus. Its members have never been very visible on the American scene but their ideas have influenced many groups of extremists. The members of Posse Comitatus believe that the American government is involved in a world wide conspiracy that wants to destroy the typical American family and to coercively subjugate the 'white race'. They are tenacious advocates of the thesis that the American government is in reality a Government of Zionist Occupation – regardless of what administration is in power – controlled by an International Jewish Conspiracy guided by a powerful group of Jewish financiers. And they believe that this conspiracy was set in motion to seize world power and deprive white Christians of their liberties, their rights, and even of their lives.[64]

7. Social polluters and powerful conspirators

Now, the various forms of right wing radicalism that I try to summarize here are found, with differing emphasizes and mixed in various ways, on many American websites like Aryan Unity,[65] Aryan Nation,[66] Storm Front White Power,[67] White Revolution,[68] Racist Joke,[69] the skinhead site Hammerskins[70] and naturally on neo-Nazi sites like Nazi Lauck NSDAP,[71] The American Nazi Party[72] and The American Nazi Party HQ – Your Reich HQ.[73] What

---

64 For more on Posse Comitatus consult the Nizkor Project available at http://www. nizkor.org/hweb/orgs/american/adl/paranoia-as-patriotism/posse-comitatus.html   [accessed 29 June 2007 (translator)].

65 Available at http://www.aryanunity.com/page1.html [accessed 29 June 2007 (translator)].

66 Available at http://www.aryannations.org/ [accessed 29 June 2007 (translator)].

67 Available at http://stormfront.org/index2.htm [accessed 29 June 2007 (translator)].

68 Available at http://www.whiterevolution.com/ [accessed 29 June 2007 (translator)].

69 Available at http://racist-jokes.com/ [accessed 29 June 2007 (translator)].

70 Available at www.hammerskins.net/.

71 Available at http://www.nazi-lauck-nsdapao.com/ [accessed 29 June 2007 (translator)].

72 Available at http://www.americannaziparty.com/ [accessed 29 June 2007 (translator)].

73 Available at http://www.pzg.biz/american_nazi_party.htm [accessed 29 June 2007 (translator)].

things are characteristic of them? A quick glance at their websites reveals that the word which crops up most is *war*. A real war, to be fought against those who are ethnically and culturally different, against those diabolical figures who are plotting the overthrow of the Western world's natural order. In a word, a war that is conducted against the Other. An Other that, in the symbolic representation that is offered the visitor, takes on the double role of *social polluter* and *powerful conspirator*. It is worth taking a moment to consider these two modes of representation.

The representation of the Other as a social polluter is widely diffused on the American sites I visited. On their webpages the Other is always metaphorically associated with 'disease' and cast as a viral presence whose very existence on American soil is sufficient to undermine its social stability and those values which have made it the place where, in the course of time, a strong and powerful nation has been built. What this amounts to is a symbolic move which aims to construct what Nils Christie has called a *suitable enemy*.[74] Who is a 'suitable enemy'? A 'suitable enemy' is a social and/or ethnic group labelled as an internal enemy that operates behind the 'lines' and is the origin of all the ills which afflict us as single individuals, as homogeneous groups and as a whole nation. The construction of this figure – which might not be simply a work of the imagination but might be based on facts which should not be generalized – serves a double function. On the one hand it serves to transform an unfocused sense of insecurity into a more concrete fear of what the members of this group do or could do. To make this clear, let's take an Italian example. Labelling works like this: some Moroccan (or Tunisian or Albanian) immigrants commit crimes, occasionally of a savage nature. *It follows therefore* that all Moroccans (or Tunisians or Albanians) are criminals. On the other hand, the figure of the 'suitable enemy' serves to strengthen cohesion inside the group that feels menaced. In a certain sense what we have here, coming into play once again, is the familiar contraposition of friend/enemy. Faced with an enemy it becomes imperative to overcome internal divisions, to reaffirm common values and to re-establish that unity which alone makes it possible to launch an effective offensive operation to defeat the enemy and throw them back beyond the social and symbolic boundaries of the group that feels menaced by this extraneous, and hence dangerous, presence.

But who are these enemies according to the American extreme right? In first place, Afro-Americans, constantly depicted as brutal and primitive, biologically inferior beings, whose very presence represents a corrosive element for the whole of American society. They are always called *niggers*

---

74 Christie, N. (1986), 'Suitable Enemy' in Bianchi, H. and van Swaaningen, R. (eds), *Abolitionism: Towards a Non-Repressive Approach to Crime* (Amsterdam: Free University Press).

and are represented as an 'external' source of social pollution and cultural decadence which clashes with the ethnic, civil and economic superiority of the white descendents of the first American colonists. In second place among the social polluters we find homosexuals. This social group represents two kinds of menace for American society. Firstly, homosexuals are always portrayed as seeking to sexually ensnare the young, above all young whites, and this behaviour, which goes against nature, threatens to undermine the religious values of the white community and their codes of socially acceptable behaviour. Secondly, homosexuals do not reproduce and thus threaten the survival of their own race. Thus they are doubly dangerous and it is necessary to oppose them in time honoured ways. In the same way as witches were once hunted down in Europe. In other words, burning at the stake is too good for them.

And this is more or less the same end promised to, or desired for, the powerful conspirators. The powerful conspirators form a category with very different characteristics to those of the social polluters. While Afro-Americans are depicted as primitive and subhuman and gays as perverts against nature, social conspirators are described as those who have power and wealth and the capacity to control. Naturally, it is easy to guess who these conspirators are: they are the Jews. There are Jews in the American government, the directors of the most important newspapers and television channels are Jews, as are the most famous scholars and university professors.[75] And all of them are united by a secret pact to set in motion a conspiracy that will enable them to dominate the world. There is a page on the National Alliance website which is illuminating on this point. It is entitled 'Great masters of the lie'.[76] I quote two brief passages:

> The reason for the lying by the media people and by the politicians and government officials is Jewish influence. Jews own or control most of the mass media in the United States, and they also own the politicians, for all practical purposes.

> Unfortunately, however, we also are inundated by lies from those who are real experts at lying, far cleverer at it than the politicians. I am referring, of course, to the Jews. They are such effective liars that we really must pinch ourselves every time one of them opens his mouth, lest we be taken in. It is, in fact, their absolutely astounding facility at lying that has persuaded me, more than any other difference between us, that an unbridgeable racial gulf separates us from the Jews. It is more than their perverse religion and more than their distinctive family life that is responsible for this facility, I am convinced.

---

75 See the 'Who rules America?' page on the National Alliance website at http://www. natall.com/who-rules-america/index.html [accessed 29 June 2007 (translator)].

76 Available at http://www.natall.com/free-speech/fs0201a.html [accessed 29 June 2007 (translator)].

I believe that it is based in their genes. From far back in prehistoric times their ancestors spent so many generations in the markets and bazaars of the Middle East changing money and buying and selling camels and goats and goods of every description, haggling over every transaction, that the ability to lie convincingly became a real asset in the struggle for survival. And it is the adverb "convincingly" that is the key here. They evolved the knack for seeming to be sincere while lying outrageously.

Thus Jews possess a great weapon with which to pursue their objective of domination: the lie. So pervasive is the use of this weapon that it has managed to twist the minds of white Christian Americans. By brainwashing them it has enabled minority groups [*sic!*] like feminists and MTV – the latter is accused to being a Jewish broadcasting channel that propagates rap and Afro-American music amongst the young – to acquire a power that is illegitimate and dangerous over all young white males.

Perhaps there is a reason that explains how it is possible that some people find such a representation of Jews credible, a reason that can be sought once again in the nature of the 'suitable enemy'. If you read but a few of the multitude of proclamations with which movements of the American far-right fill their webpages, you will notice that the portrait that they offer of the America of today is that of a country in decline. Of a country that has lost its roots, its culture and its values. A country that has been invaded by drugs at every level. A country with zero population growth as far as the white population is concerned. A country in which 'half-castes' are multiplying thanks to high immigration and a growing number of mixed marriages. A country, finally, in which whites have less and less power. And to the eyes of the American extreme right these things do not look like the product of social processes – they look like the results of machination. And this machination is anthropomorphized in the figure of the Jew as a conspirator. In this way it becomes possible to construct a symbolic narrative that transforms real social problems into a perennial conflict between distinct and clearly identifiable ethnic groups. It is a conflict that has taken dramatic forms in the past and which now seems, fortunately, weaker in intensity. But that remains alive and kicking thanks to the Internet and which, through the voices of its advocates, continues to manifest itself in all its virulence.

Chapter 4

One More Weapon:
The Use of the Web in the
Middle East Conflict

1. Islam online

Let me confess straightaway that I don't know Arabic. If I've been able to visit the websites of numerous Middle-Eastern armed groups and understand something that is because some of them are, or have a version, in English and because, in the case of sites written only in Arabic, I have been able to count on the help of Yassuf who translated their content with patience and precision.[1] Let me also add that nor am I an expert on Middle-Eastern affairs. I have the sort of knowledge that can be acquired from reading newspapers and reading some books on the subject.[2] Nothing more. After all, I am a researcher who is concerned with communication via computer and if I am delving into this area I am doing so not with the eye of a political scientist who wants to understand the political dynamics which are developing on this chessboard of war, but only with the objective of finding out what role the web has played in a war which is not conventional – in a war, that is, not between sovereign states but between states and groups which, according to Ulrich Beck's definition, have 'individualized war'.

I found these sites – as I have already said in the first chapter – in part using the Israeli site Internet Haganah[3] and its rich database,[4] which has, however, the limitation of listing mainly Palestinian sites, in part using the links on Middle-Eastern sites themselves, and finally by making use of The Hate Directory site[5] which provides a long list, with their respective

---

1   Needless to say, however, the writer alone is responsible for any errors in the following pages.

2   I limit myself to mentioning four books which I have found particularly useful: Sardar, Z. and Davies, M.W. (2004), *Islam* (Oxford: Verso); Ruthven, M. (1984), *Islam in the World* (London: Pelican Books); Burke, J. (2004), *Al-Qaeda: The True Story of Radical Islam* (London: Penguin Books); and Della Ratta, D. (2005), *Al Jazeera. Media e società arabe nel nuovo millennio* (Milan: Bruno Mondadori).

3   http://www.internet-haganah.co.il/haganah/.

4   http://www.internet-haganah.co.il/jihadi/.

5   http://www.bcpl.net/~rfrankli/hatedir.htm.

URLs, of webpages which have, in different ways, something to do with the war in the Middle East. Despite these sources, the volatility of these sites – their tendency to appear somewhere on the web, disappear for a while and then reappear in some other place with a different address – was a constant headache. Keeping tabs on them was not easy and it is probable that the addresses that I provide here, noted at the time of writing, will be different when the reader comes to read these pages.

However, I didn't imagine there would have been so many of them. As a Westerner well informed on the *digital divide*, on the digital gap between rich and poor countries and on differences in terms of access to Internet resources among and between their populations, I thought that Afghan shepherds and Iraqi mercenaries would not even be capable of turning on a computer. An awful cliché, but one that nevertheless seemed to find confirmation every time I took a look at the Internet user estimates.

Countries	% Internet users as a percentage of the whole population. An estimate.
Bahrain	21.36
Iran	0.63
Iraq	0.05
Israel	17.12
Jordan	3.99
Kuwait	9.47
Lebanon	8.38
Oman	4.42
Palestine	0.0
Qatar	9.75
Saudi Arabia	2.5
Syrian Arab Republic	0.35
United Arab Emirates	36.79
Yemen	0.09

Source: Nua Survey, How Many Online.[6]

These figures are, of course, only estimates but they give a broad indication of the situation. If we exclude the United Arab Emirates and Bahrain, two countries which do not form part of the area that interests us, and Israel for totally different reasons, there is something that is patently obvious, I said to

---

6   These statistics used to be available at http://www.nua.ie/surveys/how_many_online but are no longer published on the site [accessed 29 June 2007 (translator)].

myself. The populations of Arab countries don't have access to the Internet and so they cannot be considered a target for what is written and published on the sites of Middle-Eastern groups. So what use are they? Perhaps some cities in the area have Internet cafés where it is possible, every now and then, to consult the sites that you know, but what if the site in question disappears overnight like an inhabitant of Baghdad and you have to look for it each time? It's not as if everyone is like Salam Pax. I would have been less surprised if I had first read a few books which would have provided me with a very different picture: I refer to Fatema Mernissi's book (mentioned in the first chapter),[7] and above all to two works by Gary Bunt, *Virtually Islamic*[8] and *Islam in the Digital Age*[9] which show that already in the '90s the Internet was not solely a prerogative of the West but was also utilized in the Islamic world. Blunt says, in fact, that numerous Islamic sites have been on the web for more than 15 years – and so since well before the Second Gulf War. These are sites of a religious character and they are run by single individuals or small groups residing both in Middle-Eastern and in Western countries, that is to say, by people of Muslim faith or by Islamic religious authorities based in England, America, France and Ireland, but also in Iran, Egypt, Saudi Arabia, Pakistan or Malaysia. And they are all engaged in the work of propagating one or other of the many faces of the Islamic religion, united despite their differences in their primary objective of fulfilling their obligation, by means of the Internet, to spread Islamism – the obligation known as the *da'wah* – among both believers and those who profess other faiths. This is a duty that can be discharged in various ways and in order to understand these differences it is necessary to recall for a moment some of the characteristics of this religion, beginning with its fundamental text: the Qur'an.

The Qur'an, as many know, is a collection of transcriptions made by Muhammad's followers, in particular by his private scribe Zayd ibn Thabit, of the revelations received by the prophet through the Angel Jibreel, directly from Allah between 610 and 632AD. It is composed of 114 chapters or *surahs* of varying lengths and unlike the Bible it is not constructed as a linear narrative text nor are its verses organized chronologically according to the order in which they were revealed to the Prophet. Crudely simplifying, it can be said that rather than offering a narrative, the Qur'an conducts the reader on a journey that takes him from fundamental questions concerning 'what' and 'how' to more profound questions concerning 'why'. It does in fact

---

7 Mernissi, F. (2004), *Karawan. Dal deserto al Web*, trad. it. (Florence: Giunti, Firenze).

8 Bunt, G. (2000), *Virtually Islamic. Computer-mediated Communication and Cyber Islamic Environments* (Cardiff: University of Wales Press).

9 Bunt, G. (2004), *Islam in the Digital Age: E-jihad, Online Fatwas and Cyber Islamic Environments* (London: Pluto Press).

include accounts of events concerning the life of the Prophet and a description of the community in which he lived; it refers to the story of prophets who came before Muhammad; it makes wide use of metaphor, allegory and parables and often returns to the same theme or the same subject. It is thus a religious text constructed, so to speak, around a sedimentation of meanings which, not being grouped thematically, require interpretation. In consequence, even though parts of the Qur'an are clear, there are other parts which are not and which can only be understood through a process of exegesis, above all if you are seeking answers to problems and situations which simply did not exist in the Arabia of the seventh century. After all, this was a possibility recognized by Muhammad himself who explicitly endorsed the use of reasoned discussion in order to reach a consensual solution to controversial questions of interpretation. The process of interpretation of the more obscure passages in the Qur'an is called *ijtihad* and even if Islam does not recognize priests as having powers of intercession, over the course of time a body of experts who specialize in this work of exegesis has emerged. These are the *Ulema*, or 'the erudite'. And the Ulema have not always agreed on the meaning of important passages in the Qur'an. And nor do they today.

If to this fact we add that the Islamic religion is not at root a unitary religion but contains at least three theological roots – Sunni, Shi'ite and Sufi currents – the idea that there exists one Muslim *Ummah*, one monolithic religious community of the Islamic faith, becomes rather difficult to sustain. And Gary Bunt brings this home to the reader by listing with painstaking meticulousness, above all in the chapter entitled *Muslim Diversity online*, numerous sites which propose differing if not contradictory interpretations of the sayings of the Prophet,[10] or offer divergent teachings concerning aspects of the everyday life of the faithful,[11] or indicate diverse attitudes to take towards the followers of other religions.[12] And this is another point to underline. Let's take, for example, the problem of what interpretation to give to the term *jihad*. Today this term has come to mean – or at least this is how Westerners interpret

---

10 For example, see the following sites: Fatwa online available at http://www.fatwa-online.com [accessed 30 June 2007 (translator)], Sunnah Organization available at http://www.islaam.org [accessed 30 June 2007 (translator)], Islam101 available at http://www.islam101.com [accessed 30 June 2007 (translator)], Chishti Habibi Soofie Islamic Order available at http://www.soofie.org.za [accessed 30 June 2007 (translator)] and Islamic Awakening available at http://www.islamicawakening.com [accessed 30 June 2007 (translator)]. One site which contains a multitude of links to sites of this kind is World of Islam Portal available at http://www.worldofislam.info [accessed 30 June 2007 (translator)].

11 For example Islam Q & A available at http://www.islam-qa.com [accessed 30 June 2007 (translator)], and Ask-Imam available at http://islam.tc/ask-imam/index.php [accessed 30 June 2007 (translator)].

12 See for example the Shiachat forum available at http://www.shiachat.com [accessed 30 June 2007 (translator)].

it and how it is understood by radical Islamic groups – 'holy war' against infidels and the occupiers of Arab soil. In reality the term *jihad* indicates an effort against or in favour of many things. It is a word that comes from the Arabic root *jhd*, which indicates tension, effort, struggle, commitment and attempt. And the term *ijtihad*, that is the effort to interpret, comes from the same root. Well then, according to an accredited interpretation of the Qur'an, Muhammad distinguished two types of *jihad*: a major *jihad* to fight against yourself, and a minor *jihad* to fight against others. In short, the term *jihad* does not necessarily mean 'holy war', as it is often understood today. In reality you can have a *jihad* of the heart, of the pen, of language, of the sword and so on. Scholars and Islamic jurists have discussed the exact definition of the term for the whole of the history of Islam. And Bunt, on the basis of many documented references, says that they have not stopped doing so even now.

These were all things that I did not know when I saw the video contained in file mal7.swf,[13] the one which claimed responsibility for the 11 September 2001 attacks on behalf of bin Laden and Al-Qa'ida.[14] An ignorance which, for quite some time, prevented me from fully understanding the significance of the documents which I was accumulating in folders on my computer and which led me to catalogue them simply as 'War propaganda'.[15] War propaganda, as is well known, has three precise purposes. In the first place, it serves to keep up the morale of the civilian population by displaying victorious actions by their combatants or heroic images of their commanders. And, as we shall see shortly, there are many sites on the web which contain images and texts of this kind. In the second place, it serves to show the inhumanity of the enemy. Those long sequences of photographs which show civilian victims, their disfigured bodies, the anguish of relatives and funeral ceremonies have precisely this function. To show that the enemy is cruel and pitiless. Hence the insistence, on every website that I have visited, on the exhibition, above all, of images of children who have been killed. And of one in particular, almost always present. It depicts a child of one or two, lying naked on a small bed covered by an embroidered sheet. His skin is like marble. His lips

---

13 The video can be seen on my site available at http://www2.scedu.unibo.it/roversi/ odioinrete/mal7.html [accessed 30 June 2007 (translator)].

14 I use the term al-Qa'ida in a very conventional sense. In reality, as Jason Burke argues in the text mentioned above it is very doubtful whether an armed group of this name has ever existed. What is more likely is that a network of armed Middle-Eastern groups has existed for sometime, more or less unified, which follows al-Qa'ida, or the 'rule'.

15 On war propaganda see the two classic texts by Lasswell, H.D. (1927), *Propaganda Technique in the World War* (New York: Knopf) and Viereck, G.S. (1930), *Spreading Germs of Hate* (New York: Horace Liveright). For a review of studies of the role of the media in war in the twentieth century see Hallin, D.C. (1997), 'The Media and War', in Corner, J., Schlesinger, P. and Silvestone, R. (eds), *International Media Research. A Critical Survey* (London: Routledge).

are red and his mouth is slightly open. There are some abrasions on his body but the focus of the camera draws our eyes to a particular point: a hole the size of a coin in the middle of his stomach. A purplish-blue hole just above his belly button that is the product of a bullet that has passed right through him. A photograph, it goes without saying, of very great emotional impact for anyone who sees it. However, propaganda has also a third objective, that of undermining the morale and the courage of the enemy with threats of all kinds. In the wars of the past recourse was had to dropping propaganda materials onto frontline troops from the air or powerful megaphones were used to obsessively repeat an invitation to enemy troops to desert. Today, in the era of the Internet, resort is had to the web in order to show the whole world videos of captured Western civilians or soldiers and, if it comes to that, their killing in the most brutal of ways, or to broadcast messages which although written in Arabic are addressed to the soldiers of the Western coalition and are published in the certainty that they will be read and diffused by some Western source.

When I considered all this material more carefully I couldn't help thinking that certainly it amounted to propaganda, but not only that. And, in any case, within its limits, from a communicative point of view, it was material that had been constructed with undeniable skill. I found myself confronted with two questions to answer: What do these sites communicate and to whom? And how do they communicate it? Two questions which seem banal but answering them meant coming to terms not only with a language barrier but also with at least two other glaringly obvious circumstances. In the first place with the problem of deciphering the linguistic codes used in this type of communication and their cultural, religious and social terms of reference. And in the second place, with the fact that for the first time in history, communications concerning war use a means of transmission capable of reaching every corner of the earth and thus different audiences with not only diverse cultures but also divergent points of view with regard to the conflict in progress. In other words, they use a medium through which it is possible to literally conduct a war without limits.

Let me give you an example which will make what I mean clear. In September 2003 word got about that bin Laden had been arrested or was about to be. The Arab television station *Al Jazeera* received a video which showed bin Laden and broadcast it. In this short video all you can see is bin Laden walking, together with a companion, along a mountain path in Afghanistan.[16] He is modestly dressed. He is wearing a worn-looking light coloured tunic and, hung over one shoulder, a dark dusty cloak. He moves slowly leaning on a wooden staff, like his travelling companion. When I saw

---

16   The video can be seen on my website at http://www2.scedu.unibo.it/roversi/odioinrete/
ubl1new-1-1.wmv [accessed 30 June 2007 (translator)].

this video I thought, as I believe all Westerners did, that the message was clear: bin Laden wanted to show the whole world – all of us, both Arabs and Westerners – that he was still free and nowhere near being captured. In reality that video contained *two* messages: the first that which I had identified, addressed to Westerners. The second, much more important and completely different, was addressed to Muslims and is based on the so-called 'Muhammad paradigm'. In what does the 'Muhammad paradigm' consist? It is necessary to recall the life of the Prophet in order to understand. As is well-known, Muhammad was forced to flee from Mecca in 622, forced out of the city by its rich rulers who no longer tolerated either his refusal to submit to the secular authorities or his attacks on the cult of the idols practiced in the city sanctuary, the *ka'aba*, a cult which gave rise to a lucrative pilgrimage industry. Muhammad's flight is known as the *Hijrah* or *egira* and its importance is such that the Islamic calendar dates everything from this event. The years which followed were very hard for Muhammad, squeezed between, on the one hand, the suspicions of the inhabitants of Medina where he took refuge and the military might of Mecca on the other. But in the end he prevailed and having defeated the inhabitants of Mecca in the battle of alBadr in 624 he returned in triumph to the city of his birth where he died two years later. Now, any Muslim who thinks about Muhammad today and his flight from Mecca towards Medina – who thinks, in other words, about the *Hijra* – imagines it exactly as bin Laden appears in the Al Jazeera video. So here is the second meaning of that video. Through the video bin Laden communicates with Arab populations in symbolic terms – resorting to one of the most powerful of religious metaphors – and this is what he proclaims: like the Prophet I am in flight, but like the Prophet I will defeat the wicked and in the end I will be victorious. One and the same message but with two meanings and two objectives.

2. The electronic jihad

I will return shortly to this aspect, simultaneously symbolic and instrumental, not only of bin Laden's web communication but also that of numerous other armed Middle-Eastern groups present on the web. The question which I want to attempt to answer before I do that is that of to whom these groups address their messages. Obviously I can only formulate a hypothesis given the absence of solid empirical evidence that would permit me to go beyond a supposition but I believe that it is a reasonable supposition, based on considerations of fact. Now, in my opinion these sites have two audiences of reference. The first is constituted by Islamic populations living in Western countries. They speak, that is to say to the *Islamic diaspora*, the Islamic populations which were scattered in various epochs, in Europe and the United States. Let's have a look at the figures. According to trustworthy sources,[17] Islam has about one and half billion followers, equal to 23 per cent of the world's population, distributed over the five continents:

Islam in Africa

Region	Total Population	Muslims	% of Muslims	Muslims as % of whole
Central Africa	83,121,055	12,582,592	15.1	0.8
East Africa	193,741,900	66,381,242	34.3	4.5
North Africa	202,151,323	180,082,076	89.1	12.2
Southern Africa	137,092,019	8,935,043	6.5	0.6
West Africa	268,997,245	133,994,675	49.8	9.1
Total	885,103,542	401,975,628	45.4	27.2

Islam in Asia

Region	Total Population	Muslims	% of Muslims	Muslims as % of whole
Central Asia	92,019,166	76,105,962	82.7	5.1
East Asia	1,527,960,261	39,609,350	2.5	2.7
Middle East	274,775,527	252,219,832	91.7	17.1
South Asia	1,437,326,682	416,062,641	28.9	28.2
Southeast Asia	571,337,070	239,566,220	41.9	16.2
Total	3,903,418,706	1,023,564,005	26.2	69.3

---

17 The data presented here comes from the online encyclopedia Wikipedia, and is available at http://en.wikipedia.org/wiki/Islam_by_country. Wikipedia indicates the sources used and also provides a breakdown by country [accessed 30 June 2007 (translator)]. Information on this site is subject to frequent change.

Islam in Europe

Region	Total Population	Muslims	% of Muslims	Muslims as % of whole
Balkans	65,407,609	8,165,137	12.5	0.5
Central Europe	74,510,241	521,284	0.7	0.03
Eastern Europe	212,821,296	21,826,829	10.3	1.5
Western Europe	375,832,557	13,577,116	3.6	0.9
Total	728,571,703	44,090,366	6.1	2.9

Islam in North and South America

Region	Total Population	Muslims	% of Muslims	Muslims as % of whole
Carribean	23,809,622	15,860	0.06	0.001
Central America	42,223,849	84,035	0.2	0.006
North America	446,088,748	5,115,892	1.1	0.3
South America	371,075,531	1,014,716	0.2	0.06
Total	883,197,750	6,230,503	0.7	0.4

Islam in Oceania

Region	Total Population	Muslims	% of Muslims	Muslims as % of whole
Oceania	30,564,520	372,968	1.2	0.02

These tables confirm that Islam is deeply rooted both in North and West Africa and in Central Asia and the Middle East. But if we look at the absolute values we can see how large is the presence of people of the Islamic faith in North America and above all in Europe where this presence comes to more than 44 million people, or 6 per cent of the whole resident population. In Europe a portion of this presence is composed of people who are native Muslims, particularly in the Balkans, but all the others are immigrants. I can find no empirical research on the subject but I don't think that it is illogical to believe that some of these people make use of the Internet to visit online religious sites present in the Western countries in which they are currently resident. The utility of these sites is not otherwise explicable. And just as they can access normal religious sites – discovered by navigating from link to link, or through word of mouth or simply by using a search engine – they can arrive at the sites of armed groups. I don't believe, however, that the majority of their visitors are adults or first generation immigrants. Rather, I think that these sites are visited by their children, those who are conventionally called 'second generation immigrants'.[18] I'm not going to go into a phenomenon that has been widely studied in the academic world. It is sufficient for my purposes to repeat the hypothesis, confirmed by a considerable body of research, that it is the children of the second generation – whether born in their parent's country of immigration or arriving there at an early age in order to be reunited with their families – who suffer most from problems of integration in the new social contexts in which they find themselves. Difficulties which can lead them, as a reaction, to a sort of 'ethnic withdrawal', a closure that is cultural rather than relational with regard to the surrounding social environment and which may in turn generate an unsatisfied need of affiliation and a sense of rootedness.[19] And probably, precisely because of these characteristics, they are the ones who are the first to turn to the sites of armed groups. They are the ones, in fact, who living in the West, have easy access to the Internet and can feed their curiosity to know what their real ethnic and religious identity might be. And on the webpages of armed groups they find many things to think about. The call of the religion of their fathers. The exhibition – and the documentation – of the brutality, indeed the wickedness of the West. The humiliation, the suffering, profanation and loss of life to which those who live in their country of origin are subject. An incitement to react with violence to the bullying of Westerners. And finally, the most important message of all: we, your brothers are here, ready to welcome you. And all of this is presented in an attractive guise, which does not hesitate to call upon the support of music videos which have nothing to envy those which young Westerners can see and hear on TV channels like MTV.

Let me give you two examples which seem significant in this regard. The first is a video in Arabic hosted on a site in English called the Supporters of

---

18 This supposition is in part collaborated by the data collected by the Israeli Internet Haganah site on those accessing some Middle-Eastern sites. On this see the page at http://internet-haganah.co.il/harchives/004135.html. Only partly substantiated because while it is possible to monitor where a particular site is being accessed from, it is not possible to know who is actually accessing it.

19 See an essay by S. Allievi which is representative in this regard: 'I giovani musulmani in Europa. Tra identità tradizionale e mutamento culturale', available at http://www.comune.torino.it/cultura/intercultura/.

Shareeah.[20] It is entitled 'Come into the Jihad' and in the first part it shows, in a series of zoom shots inside houses, acts of violence committed by Western soldiers against a helpless population consisting of women, children and old people. In the second part, over a background of a ruined village, we are shown a variety of almost transparent photographs of armed militants marching with flags celebrating the Jihad. The second is a video entitled 'Songs for Palestinian children' and is hosted on the e-Jihad-net site.[21] One song includes these lines: 'Onwards Muslims, take up your swords. Palestinian children call you. Don't be frightened of death. Don't hesitate. Allah has promised you victory. Onward Muslims, take up your swords. Palestinian children call you'. And while it is sung by a chorus of voices, a stream of images scrolls past in the background depicting Islamic combatants brandishing rifles and machine guns, using rocket launchers and Molotov cocktails and burning American flags. A message that leaves no space for equivocation. At the same time, however, it is also possible to find music videos of a quite different tone like that with the English title 'Last Breath'.[22] On first hearing, it does not seem like a propaganda video. It has a tune that is very Western and catchy, and a text that is empty of any hint of fanaticism. The singer has a well modulated voice. The graphics are sophisticated and play on the visual elements to guaranteed effect. Only when you listen to it a second time paying great attention to what is being sung do you understand what it is really about.

> A chilly wind begins to blow within my soul […] And a last breath escapes my lips […] It is time to go. And I must go before it is too late. Tomorrow will be my day. It is coming. Heaven or Hell. Decide now and don't delay. My turn has come. They cry not knowing that I am before God. Let's pray instead. There is no time to stop.

Only four times in the video do images briefly appear which suggest what the text is referring to. The first shows a 'martyr' wrapped in a sort of shroud, the second a short row of bodies, the third some Arabs who are digging a grave in which to bury the dead, the fourth the title page of the Qur'an and a person who is praying. In other words this is a video which does not seek to make an immediate impact on the listener. Rather, it attempts to capture the listener with a catchy tune in order to deposit its content later, as happens

---

20 Last known address http://www.shareeah.org/enav/index. The video can be seen on my website at http://www2.scedu.unibo.it/ roversi/odioinrete/jehad.html.

21 Last know address www.e-jihad.net/ej/v4/index.php. Many music videos of this kind are available at the site Al Basrah available at http://www.albasrah.net [accessed 30 June 2007 (translator)].

22 The video is available on my website at http:// www2.scedu.unibo.it/roversi/odioinrete/videoflash.html.

with many songs which we listen to every day and which seduce us above all through their musicality. We only become aware of their words after listening to them repeatedly and only then do we understand that they have something important to tell us.

But let's move on to the second audience to which these sites are addressed. I think that it is constituted by other armed groups. If this is true, it seems to me that it is reasonable to deduce that the websites of Middle-Eastern groups form a network which has an organizational function for the various military formations which form part of it, permitting them to keep informed about each others' activities and state of health. With a limited propaganda function which is realized merely by being present on the web. Their presence on the web demonstrates, in fact, that they are no less versed than their Western adversaries in the use of the new Information technologies. I believe that this supposition is substantiated by the large number of documentary materials I have found, and in some cases downloaded, visiting these sites. Military training manuals, claims of responsibility for attacks and bombings, detailed lists of military actions undertaken, indications of possible future targets to hit: they are all to be found on these sites, both in text and in video format.

Take, for example, the Al Balsaam site.[23] Depicted in the centre of the homepage is the coffin of a (presumably) Israeli soldier wrapped in a Star of David flag and borne on the shoulders of his comrades.[24] Stamped across the image are the words 'The Jihad is the solution. We are ready'. When we enter the site the first image we are offered is that of the face of someone who has died for the cause with a green band about his head on which the ritual formula 'Allah is great' is visible. The image is bordered by a scrolling text which says: 'In the name of Allah the great and merciful. Men who believe tell the truth. Honour the martyrdom of this brother, member of the group *The Searchers of the Faith*, who died at Thot, by name Abu Aebk. May Allah receive him as a devoted martyr'. Further down, a full page image of a bullet stands out, bearing another text: 'Kill the wicked. Support the mujahideen with your prayers, money and spirit'. To the right on this same page is a link that takes you to a biography of Osama bin Laden, a classic biography which covers in chronological order the various phases of the life of the man who on this site is given the title of sheik, meaning wise man who knows the Qur'an by heart. If you click on another link a sort of forum appears where people of unknown identity exchange greetings and call for strengthened resolve in the 'the holy war' against the Zionists and the pharaoh Bush. That the American president Bush is referred to, here and on other sites, with the appellative of pharaoh is symptomatic in that it constitutes another explicit activation of

---

23 Last known address http://balsam99.jeeran.com/B_99.html.

24 A reduced version of the image is available on my website at http:// www2.scedu. unibo.it/roversi/odioinrete/balsaam.png.

the 'Muhammad paradigm'. The pharaoh is in fact he who ruled the greatest empire in antiquity and who was the leader of wicked since he opposed the realization of the divine law represented by Moses and the Jewish people, expelling them from their land. That on this occasion it was the Jews who were oppressed has no importance from the religious point of view, in fact Islam recognizes Moses as one of the prophets and the Torah as a sacred book. What is central, in this message, is only the reference to the image of the pharaoh, to the image, that is to say, of a powerful man who dared to challenge the divine law and ended up in the dust along with his empire.

The site of the Islamic Army in Iraq,[25] on the other hand, is a real war site. A surah from the Qur'an serves as an opening slogan: 'That Allah kills and tortures them with your hands. That Allah gives you victory and encourages your hearts in the way of faith'. There follows what is really and truly a war bulletin:

The soldiers of the Islamic Army in Iraq report some of the operations which took place on the 10th day of the month of Ramadan of the year 1425 of the Hijrah calendar – here summarized:

1. destruction of four British tanks and the killing of the Western soldiers who drove them.
2. destruction of a jeep and killing of driver at Baghdad.
3. destruction of 2 jeeps in the region of Aluassa and the killing of drivers.
4. destruction of tanks on the Balad road and killing of those on board.
5. destruction of a jeep at Karkuk and killing of driver.
6. killing of 4 American soldiers near Alluah.
7. destruction of 2 jeeps and killing of drivers at Ramadi.
8. destruction of a jeep and a water tanker and killing of 12 soldiers south-west of Baghdad.
9. hitting an armed vehicle on the road to Baghdad airport.
10. killing of 12 Iraq policemen in the occupied zone of Baghdad.
11. killing of more than a dozen members of the national guard in the occupied zone of Baghdad.
12. destruction of a troop transport vehicle travelling north of Baghdad.

Following this we find lists of military actions carried out on the preceding days. Always in the form of a cold communiqué: destruction of a jeep and killing of driver at Karkuk, capture of an Iraqi police officer at Baghdad and so on … In short, war bulletins whose function, I presume, is that of informing other armed groups, and perhaps the civilian population, of their military successes. One notable feature of this site is that it is possible to

---

25 Last known addresses http://iairaq.4t.com and http://www.iairaq.8k.com. An image on a reduced scale of the homepage of the site is visible on my website available at http://www2.scedu.unibo.it/roversi/odioinrete/iraqarmy.png.

enroll in a mailing list and post mail to the address enas2009@hotmail.com. A useful instrument, I should think, what is more, regularly registered with Yahoo, for keeping members informed about military feats.[26] And to show that their bulletins are not just inventions for propaganda purposes, the site also hosts a large number of videos which show military operations,[27] just as it contains a video which shows hostages – both Western and non – among which it is easy to recognize the Italian Enzo Baldoni, who, as is well-known, was tragically killed in August 2004 by one of these groups.[28] I would hazard a supposition concerning these videos: it does not seem illogical to think that they are *first* put on the web so that they can condition public opinion at an international level and *then* they are transferred to some magnetic support like a VHS cassette or a DVD disc for distribution to the local population so that they can see the military strength of these groups at first hand.

3. Al Fateh and the pedagogy of war

I now come to the second aspect of the problem, that is, to the mixture of instrumental and symbolic languages often used by these sites for communicating on the web. I will take the Al Fateh website[29] as an example, a site that the Palestinian group Hamas launched for Middle-Eastern children. To give you an idea of what it is like I reproduce a text only version in the following table:

---

26 The mailing list is still active at the moment of writing. See http://groups.yahoo.com/group/iairaq/messages.

27 One of these videos – of the blowing up of a military vehicle – is visible on my website at http://www2.scedu.unibo.it/roversi/odioinrete/capture13.mpg.

28 This video can be seen on my website at http://www2.scedu.unibo.it/roversi/odioinrete/iraqarmy.html.

29 Visible at the address http://al-fateh.net [accessed 30 June 2007 (translator)]. 'Al Fateh', in Arabic, means 'The Victorious' and this name, curiously, is identical to that of a famous comic that I read when I was small. In this context, however, the name has quite a different significance. Bear in mind, moreover, that this is a Hamas site and that many of the things I am going to list were published on the site before Arafat's death and the election of his successor Abu Mazen, who, at least at the moment of writing, is engaged in a search for a non-military solution to the Arab-Israeli conflict which is supported, though with internal dissension, by Hamas. My judgement of the site is independent of these considerations in that it is based purely on the content of the site at the moment of visiting it.

Jihadist pages		
Pictures not to forget		Friends of Al Fateh
Sheikh Hassan Salama	Magazine for girls and boys	Pictures of Palestinian children
Abu Sufyan	The best stories	Tell a friend
The martyr Omar Al Hymuny	Children of the future	Websites for children
Facts about Palestine	Heroes and the magnificent	Guest Book
Palestinian Ulema	Send us stories and poems	
A martyr's testament		
My green-fingered granddad		
Goodnight stories		

The graphics of Al Fateh do not differ much from those of the websites for children that we are used to seeing in the West.[30] In fact its graphical interface is full of cartoon figures of children and animals; there are simple clip art style images to indicate the email address or the guest book and large colourful logos which are easy to read. And like every site for children it contains different things suitable for their age. 'My green-fingered granddad', for example, is a short story which tells the tale of a boy who has a grandfather who has green fingers. When he tells his school mates they don't believe him. They insist that people with green fingers don't exist. So one day they get themselves invited to the boy's house for some tea in order to see this strange creature with their own eyes. But it is winter and his grandfather is wearing gloves. The children are disappointed and continue to make fun of him. Until the summer comes. When they return to the house a second time they discover that the boy's grandfather does indeed have green fingers. But they are green because the he is a farmer and he has just finished mowing the grass in the fields. The story ends in laughter: the mystery has been resolved.

---

30 I'm not referring to sites like Harry Potter or Disney but those created by schools, parents or the children themselves.

In much the same way, the section 'Pictures not to forget' displays a cartoon of a child wiping his brow as he sweats over his books. The text says:

Dear child, your exams are getting nearer. Don't be worried. An exam is not the end of the world and you won't be the only one who has to take them. To pass you need to make an effort. Don't trust your memory to remember what you have studied. Make a list of the most important things to remember and repeat them pretending to be in the exam. Calm yourself by sitting down and having a cup of tea.

Things begin to change a little when you visit the section 'Friends of Al Fateh'. Here the first thing we find is the message 'Dear boys and girls, you can send us your photos by post or by email'. And immediately below there are numerous photographs, each of which is accompanied by a brief message. It seems like a page from a Western kid's comic except that the tone is different. 'My name is Fatima. I'm Libyan and I wish all children a radiant future. I have a mummy and a daddy who are marvellous and I hope to have a happy life'. 'My name is Mustafà and I go to a Syrian elementary school. I dedicate all my friendship to the Palestinian children of the Intifada'. 'My name is Manal, I'm Moroccan and I am ten months old. I greet my brothers, mujahideen children'. 'We are three Syrian children. We ask God to give us victory at Jerusalem and to permit all Muslims to pray at Al-Aqsa'.[31]

Let's go on. The section 'Pictures of Palestinian children' opens with a big photograph of a child half-hidden by a sign which says 'We are not terrorists'. Underneath it is possible to scroll though a gallery of images depicting children, and only children, of four types: 1) dead children, 2) children threatened by armed soldiers, 3) children who are shooting, 4) children holding guns or pistols. I counted them: over 100 photographs and they are really upsetting. The section ends with this phrase in block capitals: 'According to Zionists these children are terrorists'.

Further on, in the section 'Send us stories and poems', I found a number of poems. I will briefly mention two of them. The first of them is called 'Why the occupation?' and it is accompanied by a photo of an Israeli checkpoint manned by armed soldiers. The text says: 'Why the imprisonment of occupation? Why the killing and the blood? What blame have the children killed by the army of occupiers? Why destroy the houses of children and their families? Why must blood be spilt? One day I will return to Jerusalem accompanied by their hands' [the reference is, I believe, given the context, to Hamas combatants]. There follows a song by Jenin, which says that it has been 'written in the blood of martyrs and is addressed to those who do nothing'. I will only quote the last line: 'I am the Intifada'.

---

31 Al-Aqsa is the second most sacred Islamic site. Israel bars men under 45 from access to the mosque.

The theme of martyrdom emerges most clearly, however, in three other sections. The first is that devoted to Sheikh Hassan Salama and is mainly historical in character though not lacking in suggestiveness or immediacy. Who is Sheikh Hassan Salama? This is explained by a biography, accompanied by a number of photographs portraying him in uniform with a chest covered with medals, which narrates the actions of a soldier who in the '30s fought against the British who had established a Protectorate in Palestine. And who died – as a 'martyr' – in defence of Jaffa in 1948, in a battle against the British troops who had been sent to defend the nascent State of Israel. The second section contains what I would call a classic Jihad tale. It tells the story of two brothers, Ma'aoh and Ma'uoh, who are depicted in a graphic style that is very similar to that of the Tex Willer comics, and of their feats during the battle of Badr. The battle of Badr was the first great battle fought by Muhammad's followers against the inhabitants of Mecca after their flight from the city. It marks the beginning of the Arab revival and it centred on an attack on a Meccan caravan in order to retrieve part of the goods which had been confiscated from them after the Hijrah. It was a violent and bloody battle, so much so that, even though the caravan managed to escape, the entire Meccan army was destroyed. The Qur'an narrates, in this regard, that at the end of the battle Muhammad gave the order that the wounded not be treated cruelly because he had been so instructed by an apparition of the Angel Jibreel. In any case, during the battle, the two brothers, Ma'aoh and Ma'uoh, wanted to kill Abu Sufyan, the Meccan military leader, who they held responsible for the death of many of Muhammad's followers. The story told by Al Fateh is rich in incident and changes of fortune but in the end the two brothers manage to kill Abu Sufyan. But both brothers claim the honour of having killed him. The story ends with Muhammad, in Solomon fashion, giving both of them the credit.

The third section, 'The martyr Omar Al Hymuny' tells the story of a young man born in Galilee in 1983. The third of eight brothers and three sisters, Omar studies in the mosque school but does not manage to complete his studies. He starts work and becomes a bricklayer. A young man of few words – that is how he is depicted – Omar venerates Jihad martyrs and has their photographs on his bedroom wall. He admires Sheikh Ahmed Ismail Yassin and Abdel Aziz al Rantissi – two Hamas leaders killed by an Israeli raid.[32] But one day something happens which changes his life. Leaving a

---

32 Concerning the killing of Rantissi, I want to quote a post which appeared on the Israeli site Internet Haganah on 17 April 2004. Title: 'The Pediatrician of Death'. Text: 'Also killed was Rantissi's son Mohammed and possibly his wife, though that remains to be confirmed. After Israel killed Hamas supreme leader Sheik Yassin, Rantissi said: "We will all die some day. Nothing will change. If by Apache or by cardiac arrest, I prefer Apache". Happy to oblige, Doc. So who's next?' This was posted by the man responsible for the running of

mosque together with some friends he is hit by a car. His friends die but he survives. Survival is a sort of revelation for him. He now understands that he must become a martyr. And he becomes one. On 24 November 2004 'Zionist' soldiers attack the house of a certain Doctor Nazaz Shahada in the Khalil quarter. Omar, together with others, rushes to defend him. A battle takes place in which the 'Islamic resistance fighters', among whom Omar, are killed. Omar becomes a 'venerated martyr' for the Islamic Jihad and is presented as such to the children who visit Al Fateh.

But Omar is not the only 'martyr' on this site. In the section 'Facts about Palestine' we find others, listed in the chronological order of their deaths. When I last visited the Al Fateh site, this section recorded those who had been killed between 28 April and 10 May 2005. The list was a short one: on 28 April the driver of a Palestinian car became a martyr when he was killed by 'Zionist' soldiers on a bridge north of the city of Khalil. Israeli soldiers had opened fire on the car in the course of its journey killing the young Palestinian. On 30 April – the list reported – two 'Zionist' tourists were hit and others were seriously injured [This was the Cairo Museum attack]. The central objective was missed, however, as the 'martyr', a young Egyptian whose name was not given, should have blown himself up inside the Museum. On 2 May an Islamic Jihad activist became a martyr after killing a 'Zionist' soldier and injuring two others north of the city of Tulkarem. It all happened in the course of an armed conflict between 'Zionist' forces and two Jihadist militants who resisted arrest. On 5 May two 16-year-old Palestinian boys became martyrs, killed by 'Zionists' in the village of Beyt Laqia northeast of the city of Ramalla when soldiers of the 'occupation army' opened fire on children of the Intifada throwing stones at their vehicles.

Finally, all that remains is for me to quote 'A Martyr's Testament', which forms another section on the site and which carries in full the letter of a Jihadist combatant written immediately before his 'sacrifice'. This is the text of the letter:

> O children of my great people, I perform this act of martyrdom in order to defend the blood of our righteous and honest people, blood which is spilt every day, indeed every hour, by the hatred of Sharon and by the Zionist army, by a hatred that has no respect for our women, our old people and our children, and for our right to a life that is free and dignified in our virtuous land.

---

the site, Aaron Weisburd. On 14 May 2004 the same Aaron Weisburd posted this message concerning Abu Musab al-Zarqawi: 'I have a suggestion for what to do with Zarqawi in the event that he's taken alive. It has something to do with a couple of tractors and some log chain. I leave it as an exercise for the reader to figure out the details'. The two posts are visible on my site at http://www2.scedu.unibo.it/roversi/odioinrete/rantissi.png and http://www2.scedu. unibo.it/roversi/odioinrete/zarq.png respectively.

We do not love death but we want to defend our honour, our land and our holy places.

We offer our insignificant souls in order to obtain security, liberty and salvation for our land, our people and our children.

Today we, the Jerusalem company of the military wing of the Islamic Jihad will make Sharon taste of the same cup that he has made us drink from every day with funeral processions for tens of martyrs, children of our people.

We promise God, the Worthy of the world, and above all our people that we will continue, as the Jerusalem company and as groups of independent resistance combatants to fight until the last occupier has left our holy land.

I offer myself – if God so wishes – as a martyr on the road of God to defend my people and my country and I say to every resistance fighter: this is the most rapid and effective choice for reaching our objectives, and that which is nearest to and most pleasing to Almighty God the Most High. For Him we will force the occupier to think again before assailing even one of our forbidden places let alone the holy places of Islam. We will take back our land.

My brothers, martyrs of the Jerusalem Battalion, Muhammad 'Abd Al-'Al, Ahmad As'ad, Dawud Abu Sawy, Sulayman Ad-Dabs and Iman Daraghna have gone before me on the road of martyrdom.

Goodbye my people. Goodbye my mother dear, my father dear and my friends. I ask you to pray for me. I will complete my task. I am proud, indeed very proud, of what I shall do: it is the only choice to take to stop the shame and affliction provoked by the enemy's planes, his tanks and his soldiers in our land.

Your brother and your son

Akram Ishaq An-nabbatiti

Jerusalem Battalion. The military wing of the Islamic Jihad in Palestine.

4. The area of conflict

Al Fateh is both a site for children and a Hamas website. Should we be surprised if we find news there of this kind? I think not and for a reason which is quite evident. It is always important to remember the context in which these sites operate. A context of war. In a war context, above all if the war is not a conventional one, what Douglas Dearth calls 'the management of perception' becomes decisive, that is to say a communicative strategy that has the objective of channelling or impeding access to a cluster of information that has been selected in such a way as to influence the emotions of a certain public, its motivations and its very mode of reasoning.[33] This is an expression which seems highly appropriate to what I have seen on

---

33 Dearth, D.H. (2002), 'Shaping the Information Space' in *Journal of Information Warfare*, **3**, p. 2.

numerous Middle-Eastern websites. But I feel that I should add something. I think that this definition becomes even more useful for understanding how these sites communicate, and in particular for how a site like Al Fateh communicates, if we add that this strategy is based on standardized modes of communication, that is to say, on a capacity to define in a precise way what the most acceptable information environment is, what its symbolic confines are and who are its most trusted promoters. In order to be successful, in other words, it is necessary that the source which transmits the message be capable of capturing first the attention and then the consensus of the receiver, providing them with content in sync with their real or potential expectations; that it process and package these messages with a symbolic wrapping that is easily recognizable and above all which is shared; and finally that its power be politically and militarily credible, a condition in whose absence it would be unable to catalyze attention or, in consequence, stabilize its communicative power in relation to its target audience.

Now, viewed in this key, a site like Al Fateh in reality does not communicate anything if by communication we mean the transmission of information. Just as little or nothing is communicated by many of the Middle Eastern sites indexed by the various agencies which are concerned with monitoring their activities from day to day.[34] It is true that there are 'war sites'. And that their function is certainly that of sending, transmitting or giving information to others, distributing messages in space to people who are nearer or further away. But for the most part it seems to me that sites like Al Fateh use communication via computer rather as a means of celebrating a great ritual. They do not perform an act involving the propagation of information so much as an act involving the representation of shared beliefs. They stage, so to speak, in a theatre consisting of millions of computers distributed all over the world but above all where the Arabs of the diaspora live, a holy ceremony in the evident hope of reuniting multitudes of people who are geographically dispersed around the idea of one great community, around the idea of one Islamic *Ummah*. In short, all they do is apply one of the most ancient and effective ways of conceiving of communication to an ultramodern technology, the Internet. As I have already mentioned more than once, when viewed as a ritual, communication takes us to terms like 'shared', 'association', 'possession of a common faith'. It exploits the archaic identity and the common roots of terms like 'communion', 'common', 'community' and, naturally, 'communication'. And this is what Al Fateh does, with its tales and its pedagogic advice coupled at the same time with a superabundance of

---

34 Not by chance the attention of these agencies is slowly but progressively shifting from the manifest content of the messages which appear in the forums of these sites to their possible 'latent' content, that is to say, to the possibility that they contain encrypted messages hidden somewhere, perhaps in the form of apparently insignificant images like an icon.

references to the religious history of Islam and the way in which it was and continues to be defended by its martyrs from military invasion by its enemies but first and foremost from cultural attack.

After all, it is precisely on this level, I believe, that many of the websites of armed Middle-Eastern groups that I have visited operate. While on the level of military conflict they attempt to affirm a power of coercion whose outcome is uncertain, through the Internet, by means of that powerful means of universal communication that is the web, they attempt to define the 'terms of the conflict', or rather what is at stake, for the benefit of both their Western enemies and 'Zionists' and the Muslim population for whom they have set themselves up as defenders and representatives. In a conventional war between sovereign states this definition of the terms of the conflict – why are we fighting and what are our objectives? – is not strictly necessary. It is useful to reaffirm it through propaganda but in reality it is always taken for granted and considered to be, rightly or wrongly, shared by the majority of the population. But on the Middle-Eastern chessboard the situation is different. What in fact do the Muslim populations which are addressed by armed Middle-Eastern groups have in common? What does a Muslim in Sudan have in common with a Muslim in Indonesia or Pakistan? An Afghan understands little or nothing of the language spoken by an Iraqi. Eating habits vary from country to country. Styles of life, above all concerning the rights of women to inherit from their husband, to personal property, to testify in court and to divorce, are different. Average earnings per head are different as are literacy rates, both inside the same country and between countries. For many illiterate Muslims the Qur'an is a collection of meaningless phrases that have to be learnt by heart in order to recite them during prayers. What can unite such diversity? What can transform this mosaic of customs, religious traditions, idioms, local practices and ethnic identities? What is the definition of the conflict that armed Middle-Eastern groups attempt to make seem evident to the eyes of all these populations to which they address appeals, letters, videos and audio messages? To me now, having visited and studied them, the answer seems clear, and my conclusion differs from the way in which what is at stake is usually defined in the West, where the thesis of the 'conflict of civilizations' is widely diffused.[35] Civilization is a term which has a precise connotation and a long semantic tradition. As sociologists who have studied its meaning in the work of Max Weber and Norbert Elias are very well aware. Their texts taught us how, above all, civilization means the creation of the State with its institutional ramifications and the consequent monopoly of legitimate physical violence as a means for the exercise of sovereignty, a system of social stratification organized according to acquisitive criteria,

---

35 This thesis was first advanced by S. Huntington (1993) in his essay 'The Clash of Civilizations' in *Foreign Affairs*, **3**.

economic and political systems whose mode of functioning is based on forms of formally codified interrelations, and integration between the various parts of the social organism and its actors thanks to the action of complex shared normative systems. There's no trace of any of this on Middle-Eastern sites. For them what is at stake is not a conflict between civilizations – the concrete institutional form of civil life – from which one should come out victorious, hegemonic. Rather, for them the terms of the conflict are found one step before and concern only the level of a 'conflict of cultures', the level of a conflict between systems of abstract values. This is, I believe, to their eyes and in their minds the only way of producing a sense of common purpose among all the Muslims of this earth. This is what can supply Iraqi, Afghani, Chechen, Indonesian, English, American or Sudanese Muslims with an identity that they can share and a sense of belonging to a cohesive community despite its being dispersed to the four corners of the earth. An imaginary community, certainly, not based on territorial proximity, with all the problems which could arise from living together, next door, from day to day, but on the sacredness of the Book, the Qur'an, on the revealed Word that has become a reason for existence.

If this is true, and it seems to me that it is, then what these websites diffuse almost obsessively is above all an appeal to a common identity of a markedly cultural character. This is the area of conflict which is constantly being mapped out anew for Muslims and infidel misbelievers by their messages. In order to do so, however, it is not sufficient to master Western technology, or become experts in the construction of webpages and in the management of network connections, though these skills would not be misplaced in someone who is concerned with the online presence of these websites. Above all, it is necessary to be effective communicators or to try to be so, communicators capable not only of transmitting messages that are convincing but, first and foremost, of doing so in the language which is the most efficacious possible. And it is from this point of view that you can not help noticing a constant recourse to high profile communication techniques. That Osama bin Laden is a great communicator is by now widely recognized even in the West. But why is he? What is his winning move? Not certainly the fact that he is a military commander – or if you prefer, an instigator – in the front line (if he is) – blessed with innate charisma. Many other mujahideen commanders who operate on the Middle-Eastern chessboard are. Because he is astute in choosing the time and modes of his appearances and pronouncements? Certainly this is a gift that deserves recognition, and he must have acquired it from his time in the West. But his real professionalism as a respected communicator comes above all from his use of two oratory techniques which he shares with many other voices on the web and which transform what he says – whether true or false – into an enchanted narrative which seizes the attention of the listener and is convincing – I repeat, regardless of its content. These two techniques consist in repeated reference to passages in the Qur'an and recourse to classical Arabic.

It is not necessary to be very subtle when sending messages to the West. It is sufficient to show the video of the beheading of a hostage and your object is achieved. Or to equal effect you can publish somewhere a sort of manifesto or programme like the famous 'Letter written by the wife of a martyr to the wife of Paul Johnson' that appeared in an issue of the magazine Sawt al-Jihad (Voice of the Jihad) and was taken up by many organs of the International press, and which I quote in its entirety below:[36]

THE BLOOD OF YOUR HUSBAND IS THE BLOOD OF A DOG BECAUSE HE IS AN IDOLATROUS INFIDEL

I have heard that you appeared on television feigning innocence and wondering haughtily what was your husband's sin and what was his crime. I believe you are not ignorant of the fact that he was one of the greatest criminals indeed, although he is not considered that according to your standards, you infidels. For you call the criminal innocent and the innocent one, defending his rights – criminal. Or else, what was the purpose of your husband's work with the Apache helicopters? Have you ever believed that these helicopters hover over Afghanistan, Palestine, and Iraq to shower flowers and sweets over the heads of our children there? Or do you know that they throw on them rockets and bombs in order to turn their streets and homes into ashes upon which their corpses become coal? Is his work above reproach, then? Or was he innocent, while he worked on this kind of airplane ?

Do you know that my husband was killed before my eyes in his homeland? Do you know that those who killed him are security people trained to defend the imperialists and to frighten and kill the Muslim people of the country? When your husband was taken hostage, there was much talk and the world was shaken. However, these same people did not speak half as much when America, the so-called country of justice and liberty, has been detaining more than 600 Muslims in Cuba for the past three years. That is besides our prisoners in Iraq, Pakistan, the land of the Two Sacred Mosques [l'Arabia Saudita, n.d.r.], Jordan, and other places.

You should know that our brethren whom you detain in your prisons and our brethren whom your husband used to burn with his helicopters are not alone. Rather, there are hearts pounding with love for them, just as you have demonstrated that you have loved your slain husband. Nay, we love them more than you can imagine because the blood of a Muslim is for us more precious than the Ka'ba, but the blood of your husband is the blood of a dog because he is an idolatrous infidel.

---

36 Source: *The Guardian*, http://www.guardian.co.uk/elsewhere/journalist/story/0,7792, 773258,00.html.

THE CORPSE OF YOUR HUSBAND SHALL BE FOLLOWED BY MOUNTAINS OF CORPSES

Do you know that we have not done anything [yet] about the blood of Muslims and the blood of my husband that was shed for no reason. We are just getting started and the corpse of your husband shall be followed by mountains of corpses of his countrymen, until they leave the country of our Prophet, Allah's prayer and peace upon him, lowly and humiliated. How can you claim innocence for your husband, Allah's curse on him, while you have been hearing the warnings of the Mujahideen calling you to leave our country that is forbidden for you? You however shut your ears and went obstinately with your wrongdoing. This is your penalty. May you shed tears mixed with blood, just as we wept blood because of your airplanes and your troops.

When my husband was killed you certainly were not interested, nor did you know about it; and if you had known, you probably would have been pleased that he was killed before he reached your husband and his countrymen. However, I find solace in the fact that the Mujahideen were able to reach their target with precision, and they killed your husband by slaughtering him. By Allah, on that day I rejoiced a lot because the real terrorist was killed having been gorged with the blood of our Muslim children.

WE HATE YOU, INFIDELS, AND WE LOATHE YOU TO THE BONE

I don't know whether you know that we hate you, infidels, and we loathe you to the bone. How could we not, while you are given preference over us even in our own country? For a long time did one of our airplanes hover to search for your husband while he was held hostage? There was much talk – even by people who pretend to be Muslim clerics – about negotiating with the Mujahideen, in order to persuade them to set your husband free. But my husband, they prevented us from praying over him, even after his death, and they did not give us his pure body for burial. We rely only on Allah to punish those who wronged us for the purpose of pleasing your husband and his likes. None has uttered a word about my husband even though everybody knew my husband and attested to his righteousness. That was because of fear of their goddess, America.

Tell the government, which has appointed itself over us, that what they do with our youth who are engaged in Jihad is good: If you kill them, you thereby send them to heaven in the shortest way, Allah willing; and if you let them stay alive, not having overcome them, that is fine for they will fight you and will force out the infidels form the land of Islam.

Or else, you can be even more explicit and write a communiqué like that with which the self-styled 'Secret group of the Al-Qa'ida organisation in Europe' claimed responsibility for the July 2005 London bombings:[37]

> The secret group of the Al-Qa'ida organisation in Europe.
>
> In the name of Allah, the merciful, the compassionate. May peace and blessings be upon the victims of the killings in our sacred land and on Our Lord Muhammad. Allah's peace and blessings be upon him.
>
> The community of Islam, rejoice. The community of Islam, rejoice. It is time to take revenge against the British Zionist crusader government. We have replied to the massacres perpetrated by Great Britain in Iraq and Afghanistan. Today our heroic mujahideen have carried out a blessed action in London and now Great Britain is trembling with fear and terror in the north, in the south, in the west and in the east.
>
> We have repeatedly warned the Government and the British people. Today we have kept our promise and we have carried out a blessed military action in Great Britain after numerous attempts by our heroic mujahideen.
>
> We say to the Governments of Denmark and Italy, and to all the crusader Governments, that they will be punished in the same way if they do not withdraw their troops from Iraq and from Afghanistan. With this message we have warned you.

5. Prophets and pedagogues of holy war

But when you want to address your fellow believers it is necessary to use a different language and tone. Which? You can see it on a site like Saaid.net,[38] a site in Arabic which is clearly addressed to an Islamic audience. What do you find on this site? First of all, let me quote a part of the subject index:

> Before principles are swept away
> Don't despair Baghdad
> From Mustafa Latifi al-manfulaty to the heroes of Islam in Iraq
> Muslims, unite, the community calls upon you
> To Fatima of Iraq
> Falluja and the sweetness of victory
> How they will manifest themselves to you
> Letter asking advice for Iraqis addressed to the scholars of the community
> From Ghazuny to Kandahar to Falluja: the cities fall but there is no God but God

---

37 I found the full text in Arabic on the Der Spiegel homepage the following day. It is available at http://www.spiegel.de/politik/ausland/0,1518,364121,00.html [accessed 30 June 2007 (translator)].

38 Last known address http://saaid.net/mktarat/jeahd.htm.

Where is Al-Zarqawy
A group of learned Yemenites sustain the fatwa of the learned Saudis against
Iraq
Counsel of dignity and nobility

These and other materials are all presented in both textual form and in the
form of video or audio files. I puzzled over this duplication and I think that
I have found the reason for it. The managers of the site – at least, this is my
hypothesis – know that only some of those whom they are addressing are
literate. Hence the need to offer their messages in two different formats. The
first, textual, is for those who are capable of reading what is on the site for
themselves, the second, video or audio, is utilized so that messages can be
downloaded and transferred to a VHS cassette or a simple audio cassette and
thus be listened to on an ordinary cassette player by anyone, wherever they
are. In short it is a method which ensures that their messages can be distributed
widely and relatively rapidly among the whole civilian population, even the
least cultured and the most distant.

But how are Saaid.net's messages constructed? Let's take, as an example,
the first that appears on the site and which is entitled 'Before our principles
are swept away'. It is a long extract and it is not clear to whom it is addressed,
but it is worth reading all the same.

> Praise be to Allah Lord of the two worlds. Victorious for believers and a humiliator
> for misbelievers. Praise be to Allah who has shown us the way to Islam and has
> guided us on the road of Truth. I bear witness that there is no God but Allah. He is
> unique and has no associates, and I bear witness that Muhammad is a servant of
> God and his messenger. He was sent by Allah to guide us on the road of the true
> Religion and to show us all his Religion. Lord, Peace and Blessings fall on our
> Prophet Muhammad and on His Family, on His Companions and on those who
> will be well guided on the Day of Judgement.
>
> The Highest has said:
> *'O you who believe, if you revert from your religion, then God will substitute in
> your place people whom He loves and who love Him. They will be kind with the
> believers, stern with the disbelievers, and will strive in the cause of God without
> fear of any blame. Such is God's blessing; He bestows it upon whomever He
> wills. God is Bounteous, Omniscient'* (Qur'an, Surah 5, The Feast, Verse 54).
> What can I write with ink that is sufficiently severe against the imposters who
> have betrayed the teaching of our fathers and have wounded us? What can I write
> against the impertinence of those who usurp the robes of wisdom? Have the Wise
> fallen? Have they abandoned the people of the jihad? What can I write when the
> enemies of our community and of our religion collaborate with the Crusaders and
> with the Jews and with hypocrites like Ahfad Ibn 'Alqimy and attack the spiritual
> leaders of the community, their paladins and the lions of the frontier?
>
> Should I waste my words on the imposters? Use the ink of my pen against the
> enemies of the community, against the Crusaders, the Jews and their collaborators?

May my written words be against this group that make propaganda for the path of the forefathers but do not walk down it, this group that imitates the great spiritual leaders of our community but betrays them! This group is not coherent with what it says and does. It mixes poison with the honey. It has extracted a rusty sword against the true sages and those who command the heights of Islam. They claim the glory of waging a holy war and they have abused it. They defend respect for the sages and they have cursed them. They support unity but they have divided and injured us. They have kept quiet saying "perhaps" and "but" and they have remained in silence before the Devil. My brother, I will not join them in their silence in these dramatic days. I must talk even though they will not like it.

I must write my words against these imposters since they are a danger to our community. I must talk to you, my brother, because they have also appeared in the Land of the Two rivers after the occupation of the new Crusades, and since then we have begun to hear things which are strange and new, which differ from the principles in which we were educated and which were taught to us and which we have heard from the learned men of our community like the Imam Ibn Baz, 'Othmain, Fuzan, Jabrin and many others.

Allah is saddened by what this group says about Him to our persecutors and to the people of Sunna, and by what they say about Him to those who contribute to the occupation, to the guilty and to the collaborators. Allah is saddened that this group forms part of those that command the people of Sunna and amongst them the people of Iraq. Perhaps their truth will arrive for all in our community but why remain in silence when they try to impose themselves on our sages?

Why remain in silence when they attack the mujahideen?

Why remain in silence when they replace the true with the false and they stray from the sayings of our esteemed scholars?

Why remain in silence when we see them at the side of misbelievers or of the godless, they who use words to judge our scholars and who abandon the mujahideen?

My brother in Allah, I write this while I hear the sound of airplanes and cannons. Are those who have sold themselves when it was necessary to face up to the Crusaders and their collaborators my brothers? Are they my brothers who mock respect for religion, sully the words of the Lord of the Two Worlds, and rob, kill and drive away Muslims? I say and write my words in these circumstances. This is a letter to the scholars of our community and to its leaders. Perhaps they understand these lies and can clearly see the errors and the dangers that bear down on the young people of our community and on the future of our religion in an epoch in which it is attacked by the claws of other communities.

My brother in Allah, I want you to remember these simple facts. They have abandoned the jihad and not only that. They deny every call to the jihad, they deny the American danger and that of its allies. They have come to the point of writing books like the scholars. These misbelievers refuse to support the jihad in occupied Muslim countries. Their words do not warn Muslims against the domination of misbelievers. On the contrary. They avoid concerning themselves with misbelievers. They invite people to abandon the road made by our forefathers and at the same time they claim to be its protectors. They give the young controversial books which question our principles, and if they fall prey to a fratricidal war they claim to have warned them against the war and against unbelief. The moment has come for them to return to the order of God and of His Prophet – peace and the blessings be with Him.

Servants of Allah! With these words I do not write anything that you have not heard from them. I write these words about facts that we ourselves are living and of which we are witnesses. How many times have we sat in assemblies and heard them? They want to stop the jihad in Iraq, in Chechnya, in Afghanistan and in Palestine. They say that the jihad is a fratricidal war. Don't be surprised, my brother, if I say this. They deny and repudiate Muslim commentary and haven't we heard that they have put together or written books which warn Muslims against the supremacy of the unbelievers? Why aren't we aware of it? Why do they use their impertinent language against their brothers in faith and against the mujahideen? Sometimes they are against terrorism, other times they want to attack the Sultan. And on another occasion they are with the unbelievers, with precisely those who have unleashed the discord of unbelief. Why do they not talk of the crimes committed by the Crusaders in the prisons? Why do they not talk of the danger which hangs over us? Why do they not talk of the massacre of innocents? Why do they not spur the young to prepare themselves, and I do not mean only for the jihad? Where are their words when important questions are talked of? Where are their words on that civil war that the occupation of Muslim countries has become? Where are those sheiks of Islam, Ibn Taymiyya, Ibn Kathir, Ibn alqiyyim and Dhahaby? Did they not perhaps talk of the danger when it struck the land of the Muslims, did they not perhaps talk in their books and in the sermons of an imminent danger? Did they not perhaps talk of the duty of the jihad? Did they not perhaps talk of a jihad against those that collaborated with the enemy? Or is our epoch perhaps unlike theirs?

Servants of God, those of whom I speak are not convinced by this, they have left the path. Some days ago I read an article by an Ulema in which those who did not agree with the other scholars were charged with dealing in lies. A traitor to the tradition had distributed a book called 'The Iraqi Questions' which concerned questions of faith and unbelief. This book was falsely attributed to the Ulema Al-Fuzan. After it came out discord broke out in Iraq because there were many errors in the book and young Iraqis began to polemicize about this and that, but Allah be praised, the truth about that book became clear when the Ulema Al-Fuzan denied having written it. But what a disgrace! Did they perhaps withdraw that book or refute it? No my brother, indeed they made it the object of discussion and of apologetics whose reasoning I cannot accept – but we are of God and to Him we will return.

My brother, I do not want to talk of imposters who discuss questions of dogma because it is disgraceful, but I beg of our scholars that they make truth triumph and fight those who oppose it before our principles are swept away and its framework smashed.

God guide us to Truth

God guide us towards that which will not make us stray

God give victory to your Book and to the tradition of your Prophet

God protect our scholars from error

God give victory to our brothers the mujahideen in their struggle against unbelievers

Peace and blessings on our Prophet Muhammad, on His Family and on all His Companions

Why is the linguistic form of this letter interesting? It is interesting because its author writes in a cultured language – something that will of the nature of things not be evident in an English translation. More precisely, it is written in classical Arabic. Conflict is always called jihad, the enemy is a kafir, an infidel, or is represented in terms of an alliance between Crusaders and Jews. The letter opens with a ritual invocation and a quotation from a surah. The whole letter, in short, is deliberately constructed with recourse to a symbolism that derives from the Qur'an and to a religious terminology that is rarely employed in the common language but that the author is certain will be interpreted by his reader as conferring indisputable authority because its use is the prerogative of the few.

It is this mixture of classical language and Quranic terminology that gives messages of this kind, whether in written or audio format, a persuasive force that it is difficult for a Westerner to imagine. And it possesses a persuasive force that it is difficult to imagine because Westerners have long lost the habit of dealing with the power of charisma. It seems to me, though, that in order to understand the persuasive power of the communications of armed Middle-Eastern groups via the web, particularly if those who declare their intentions, their projects and their rules are 'men of culture' like the writer of the letter above, it is necessary to draw precisely on the concept of 'charisma', not in the weak definition offered by everyday language but in the strong definition of the term provided by, for example, Max Weber.[39] What in fact does Weber say about charisma, a key concept in his sociology since it enables him to highlight some defining aspects of the modern world, and a concept to which he often returns in his work? I will try to summarize what he says in a few lines. Now, according to Weber, charisma, or better, the exercise of the power of charisma is closely tied to the theme of secularization and loss of contact with a transcendental dimension.[40] Nietzsche, in the same years in which Weber writes his works, celebrates the equally famous 'death of the gods', an affirmation that Weber takes up but does not share. For him the gods are not dead, rather they have withdrawn into the more hidden corners of individual consciousness. As a result of the secularization of everyday life the religious dimension has become something eminently private, to practice in the

---

39 Weber, M. (1978), *Economy and Society* (Berkeley: University of California).

40 Op. cit. See also Weber, M. (1966), *Il lavoro intellettuale come professione*, trad. it. (Milano: Einaudi), p. 19, foll.

shadow of the church, in the solitude of a personal and exclusive relationship between the individual and his God. In other words, according to Weber, with the coming of modernity the gods have lost their exclusive power to give a sense to the world and its becoming, as was, on the contrary, the case in the ancient world, when they and the system of values they represented gave men a collective vision of their existence and essential points of reference for action. What is good and what is evil? What is right and what is unjust? What is the meaning of life and of death? These questions, Weber says, once found answers in the transcendental dimension of religion, that is to say, in a system of shared beliefs and values. Then things changed. Above all, the development of science, with its cargo of rationality, has slowly displaced religious systems as interpretative paradigms of earthly reality and has taught us to look at the world around us in a different way. The enchantment of the world has been shattered, the solid tie between men and the religious spirit has been cut and what has taken its place is a hard core of calculating rationality. Scientific laws have taken the place of magical interpretations of historical becoming, and rational calculation has become the basis of a great part of human action. So, indeed, behaves the capitalist entrepreneur who rationally calculates profit and loss and who is perpetually in search of an optimal combination of factors of production that will provide him with a profit that is cyclically reproducible. His economic actions are no longer, as they once were, directed *ad maiorem gloriam dei*. Likewise the professional politician, no longer a carrier of strong values as in the time of the prophets, has become a bureaucratic operator who moves in a forest of codified procedures, legal documents, laws and clauses with the one objective of making a living from this activity. The politician – as Weber says in a famous passage – has become not he who lives for politics but he who lives off politics.[41] In other words, he is an individual without charisma. While the true politician, he who is able to shake to its foundations the 'iron cage' in which the advent of rationalism threatens to imprison our social systems as a result of its innate tendency to bureaucratize every form of human action, is distinguished precisely by his possession of this quality, a quality that makes him an heir, however diminished, of the ancient prophets. Charisma is not in fact synonymous with personal charm, with the capacity to tell tales or with marked sensibility. Rather, these characteristics are consequences which derive from the possession of an extraordinary quality that manifests itself in the form of an annunciation: 'It has been written but I tell you …' An annunciation that is a proclamation of a radical change. One that concerns, above, all the sphere of values. All prophets – Weber continues – have begun their work of renovation with this announcement and they remain faithful to

---

41 Weber, M., *Il lavoro intellectuale come professione*, op. cit. p. 57.

it at all times. They are therefore simultaneously innovators and combatants. They announce a message which affirms the necessity or the duty of rewriting the Tables of the Law and in order to accomplish this they are prepared to fight even at the cost of their lives.

But these objectives cannot be achieved by one man alone. The prophet needs a faithful following, a handful of devotees at first, then a mass of followers, who believe in his annunciation, make it their own, and take upon themselves the task of spreading the Word to the four corners of the earth. The prophet and his following thus share the same faith and form a spiritual and religious community, but in order for this to happen certain conditions must be fulfilled. The announcement of a new gospel is not sufficient in itself. The prophet must convince his followers that the Word which he makes flesh is valid and legitimate. That is to say, he must exercise a charisma that is persuasive. On the one hand he has to demonstrate that the exceptional qualities that he has displayed are not transitory, destined sooner or later to disappear, but are intrinsic to his very nature. His charisma must transform itself, in other words, into an authority that is collectively recognized and which he personifies. Hence, the constant recourse, in the ancient world, to the performance of miracles. Making the blind see and the crippled walk, healing the sick. On the other hand the prophet must ensure that his message is not distorted in the course of its transmission to his followers. And from this point of view, the prophet emerges as more of a teacher than a tyrant. He teaches, he does not impose. He uses the word, not the whip. He explains, illustrates, associates, resorts to parables and metaphors, tells exemplary tales, frames questions and supplies answers. In his everyday work as an educator of a community of believers he seeks to construct, in a way that is intelligible, a new and coherent vision of the world in which every human experience finds its precise collocation and its significance is clearly defined. It cannot be incomplete or imprecise. It can avoid detail, but the organization of the symbolic structure that he patiently constructs must contain within it all the connections and references necessary to permit someone who has absorbed it to descend without too much difficulty from the general to the particular and to ascend, inversely, from the everyday to the transcendental and find a meaning.

Now, it seems to me that a Weberian reading of charismatic power constitutes a very useful basis for understanding the communicative modes employed by many armed Middle-Eastern groups and their more visible exponents, and perhaps also for understanding the political culture which underpins their strategy of action – the latter, though, is a subject that I willingly leave to political scientists. Useful, but it also brings us to a paradoxical question: is it possible for charisma to be digital? Is it possible to exercise charismatic power over someone, indeed over a mass of people, not through direct relations of a widely diffused nature, as once happened, but in a mediated way, through the use of a communication technology which many consider poor because it happens in the absence of interlocutors? Would the 'Sermon on the Mount' have had the same resonance and been as effective if it had appeared on a website instead of being proclaimed on a hill in Galilee? Well, paradoxical though the question may be, Weber himself supplies an answer when he says that charisma is not a phenomenon of the past that modernity and the secularization of our social systems have eliminated forever from the stage of history, but something that can reappear and in fact reappears every time that transcendental values – whatever their content – are proposed anew by a messenger. By this I don't mean obviously to associate bin Laden or the many Ulema who have issued proclamations in promotion of the jihad with the prophets of antiquity, or to argue that they are their modern reincarnation, but it seems that what they attempt to do, making skillful use of the new technologies, is to cast themselves in the eyes of the Arab masses as the present day accredited progeny of those charismatic figures, as the legitimate heirs of a Prophet recognized as such by tradition and whose teaching and doctrine they undertake to propagate and defend.

If this is true, then the quotations from the Qur'an, the recitation of surahs and the references to the holiness of Muhammad all appear in a different light. They are not merely rhetorical expedients with which to deceive the desperate and often illiterate masses, the 'damned of the earth', rather they form an argumentative framework with which to give more vigour and credibility to a very simple message that is addressed to the Arabs of the world: remember who you are. Remember where you come from. Remember your customs. Remember your laws. Remember your religion. And behave accordingly. In short, what these sites provide on a daily basis is an exercise for the memory. It would be wide of the mark to reduce this exercise to brainwashing, as many authoritative commentators from the West have done. Brainwashing means transforming a given personality into another, completely different from that which preceded it. It means changing a person's system of values, his beliefs, his points of reference and his ways of conceiving of interpersonal relations, with the objective of obtaining a behaviour different from that which is habitual to him. 'Become different': that is what brainwashing wants. What the pedagogues of holy war write and say is very different: 'Become what you are'.

6. Part for the whole

But however powerful and persuasive their incitements, the pedagogues of holy war have a weak point. A weak point that should be honestly recognized by those who refuse to call them 'terrorists' and who think that they are 'resistance fighters' against an occupation that is unjust and cruel. And this is the fact that they do not tell the whole truth. Even if we admit some truth in it, theirs is a half truth. To what must true Muslims return according to the scholars who sustain the jihad? To what culture must Islamic peoples return in order to recreate that order which originally governed their communal lives? They must return to the words of three sacred texts: the Qur'an, the Shari'ah[42] and the Hadith.[43] They must return to the Five Pillars of Islam: the Shahadah, the profession of faith according to the formula 'There is no God but Allah and Muhammad is his Prophet';[44] Salah, or ritual prayer, which must be performed five times a day; Zakat, the obligation to give alms to the poor; Sawm, or fasting during the month of Ramadan; and the Hajj, the pilgrimage to Mecca. But on sites like Saaid.net, and on many other similar sites that I have visited, I have never heard nor read of anything else. Even in the face of massacres and tragedy:

Never have the things we have heard on the battlefields where Muslims and Infidels fight seemed strange to us.

Allah's words never seemed strange to us: "If there are twenty of you who are steadfast, they can defeat two hundred, and a hundred of you can defeat a thousand of those who disbelieved. That is because they are people who do not understand" (Surah of The Spoils of War, verse 65).

It never seemed strange to us that three hundred Muslims should fight an enemy three times that number.

Bira' Bn Malik's deeds when Musaylima rebelled in the fortress of the high walls never seemed strange to us. He said in the battle: "Put on my armour, load me in a catapult and fire me into the fortress. If I am not killed I will open the doors to you". They did as he asked and he fell upon Musaylima's thousands of soldiers like a flash of lightening. Fighting alone he killed tens of them. He had to ward off eighty blows to open the doors and then the Muslims entered and killed Musaylima and his men.

It never seemed strange to us that Thabit Bn Qays dug a hole in the ground to hide and that when he faced his enemies he killed many before dying.

Yes, it never seemed strange to us to see with our eyes and hear with our ears how groups of believers maintain their commitment to God, defend their goods, their land and their religion and annihilate the arrogance of the strongest States in the world with their planes, their soldiers and their tanks.

Ja'far has said: "How beautiful is paradise and its surroundings. The drinks are good and fresh. The avidity of the Byzantines takes them nearer to the torment of the distant darkness".

---

42 Literally 'the path leading to the watering place'. The Shari'ah is the book of Islamic law, compiled and codified by the great Muslim jurists of the eight and ninth centuries.

43 This text is a compilation of the sayings attributed to the Prophet Muhammad – as opposed to divine revelations dictated by him.

44 To which Shi'ite Muslims add 'and Ali is his Friend'.

Here is Falluja, where your brothers are! The Falluja of sacrifice and of nobility. What greater nobility than that of children from whom a mother has been torn and that of children from whom the land has been torn.

Here at Falluja the water of life is drunk and the true sun shines. At Falluja the leaves of hope gleam.

Here at Falluja holy angels rise with the souls of martyrs and upon them descends the grace of the Merciful One.

Here at Falluja there is the fragrance of musk for he who has known misery and there is the fragrance of jasmine for he who has smelt the perfume of Paradise.

Here at Falluja there is a school of life for he who has desired life and a school of Paradise for he who has aspired to Paradise.

Falluja you have been an example to me.

You have taught me that in my community there is still pride and generosity.

You have taught me that we can do anything if we are united, if we embrace death and we offer our lives to the Lord of the two Worlds.

You have enabled me to discover that the blood of Muslims, worthless to the people of the Earth, is rich for the people of Heaven.

You have shown me that in my community the heart beats still, tears run and the body challenges sleeplessness and fever.

You have removed the darkness from our hearts, the blindness from our sight, the deafness from our ears and indolence from our limbs. And now in he who does not see, does not hear and does not move, the words of the Highest One sound: "Had God known of any good in them, He would have made them hearers. Even if He made them hearers, they still would turn away in aversion" (Surah of The Spoils of War, verse 23).

You Martyrs of Falluja, heroes who have given us an example worthy of our ancestors, you who have repelled the enemy and inspired in us a love for sacrifice, when you meet the Merciful One and enter Paradise, ask forgiveness for those who call upon Him since you would not have crossed the river and taken this road if we had not been with you in our hearts, our souls and in our prayers.

You, heroes of Falluja, you have chosen the shortest road to Paradise.

Is this all there is to Islam at it origins? Is Islam only an unlimited hatred for the infidel, celebration of martyrdom, stories about Mecca and religious formulas? This is what the pedagogues of holy war would have their audience believe with their rhetorical fabulations which are transmitted via television to the whole world and diffused via the web by the great galaxy of extremist Islamic sites. But even if it is agreed that Islam was originally fabricated from such materials, these materials only form a part of a much wider, richer and more intricate cultural universe. Instead, the pedagogues of holy war pass off this part for the whole. Indeed they claim that this part is the whole. In so doing they remove – they who appeal to memory – the complexity, the dynamism, the counterpointing of meanings and points of view which are the real richness of any culture, and thus also of Islamic culture, given that they are the result of its history and of the stratification of values, scientific knowledge and symbolic content which every epoch has deposited over that preceding it, in part transforming and in part conserving the collective consciousness of a people. In short, the supporters of the jihad should talk about something quite different if they want to remind their people that they have a cultural identity that is strong and undeniable. An identity which can in no way be reduced only to the heroic gestures of martyrs and jihadists. In its construction men whose greatness is measured according to other criteria have participated. Men who were philosophers – I have never seen the name of Averroes mentioned on any Islamic site and yet he is an author studied in every high school in the world. Men of letters – who has not read any of the stories in 'A Thousand and One Nights', the story of Shahrazade who tells a tale a night to her king Shahryar in order to save her life, written by the Arab al-Jahshiyari in the tenth century? Men who were mathematicians – is not the system of numbers we use today, to give the most banal of examples, of Arab derivation? Who introduced the zero if not the Arab mathematician Muhammad Bin Ahmad? Who invented algebra if not the Arab al-Khwarizmi? Men who were astronomers – who named many of the stars, even in our skies, if not Arab astronomers? Who wrote a treatise on the heavenly vault which supplied Dante with the basis of his astronomical knowledge if not the Islamic scholar al-Farghani? And one could go on. It would be a very long list, which would fill many pages.

But of their names and of their achievements the pedagogues of holy war never make mention. For them they simply do not exist. They prefer to propose with a monotonousness which is deafening the bloody mantra of the jihad and the killing of the infidel, their archetype of spiritual greatness. But I believe that there is another reason for this silence. If they told the truth, if they narrated the history that has made the world of Islam truly great and in the name of this indisputable greatness they were to ask for that recognition of their rights and merits which is their due, the vision of the world which they are attempting to diffuse among the Arab masses of the Middle East and of the diaspora in the West would collapse like a castle of cards built by an inexpert hand. In other words: they would strangle themselves with their own hands.

But this has not happened. A caricature of Islam which does not reflect its essence continues to be diffused on a planetary scale through the Internet and the webpages of armed Middle-Eastern groups. I would add, but this is a personal conviction, that if this caricature has put down roots in the Western imagination this is because it has been able to count on the prominence it is given on a daily basis by traditional Western media. The press and television, in particular, never lose an opportunity to inform us of every threat made by bin Laden and Al Zarqawy or of the latest filmed decapitation of some 'infidel' that has been posted on the web. Motivated by a duty to keep us informed. I can't quarrel with that. It is an inviolable duty that lies at the base of any democratic society. But it would not be a bad thing if these same means of communication were to come to grips, every now and then, with another reality. The sites I have attempted to describe in these pages are not the only sites on the web. Slowly the web is being populated also by other presences. Presences which are significant because they show that there are people and social groups who do not only look back to the past and to tradition but who have an eye for the future of an Islamic society that is changing with the times, that is complex and full of inevitable contradictions. Sites like Al Minbar[45] which does not offer Quranic sermons but analysis and political discussion and on which everyone is free to express their point of view. Or like Arab Net.[46] Or the sites listed by Fatema Mernissi. The sites of Arab women like Arab Women Connect,[47] Karamah[48] or Huma Ahmad's site.[49] Sites like the Iraqi Linux User Group which tries to diffuse the Open Source culture in a country still racked by war.[50] There are many Iraqi[51] and Iranian blogs[52] which narrate, analyse and debate, with a liveliness and a freshness which leaves nothing to be desired with respect to Western blogs. In short, an attentive and patient exploration of the web would reveal just how many Arab voices there are which have something to communicate other than surahs from the Qur'an. The problem is whether you have the desire and the opportunity to take time to listen or whether you prefer to think that the only voice that is worthy of attention is that which talks monotonously and repetitively only of death and destruction.

---

45 Available at http://alminbar.itgo.com/forum.htm [accessed 30 June 2007 (translator)]. Al Minbar in Arabic means 'The pulpit'. This site (in French) should not be confused with other sites of the same name like http://www.alminbar.net.

46 http://www.arab.net [accessed 30 June 2007 (translator)].

47 http://www.arabwomenconnect.org [accessed 30 June 2007 (translator)].

48 http://www.karamah.org [accessed 30 June 2007 (translator)].

49 http://www.jannah.org/sisters/ [accessed 30 June 2007 (translator)].

50 http://iraqilinux.org [accessed 30 June 2007 (translator)].

51 See http://iraqblogcount.blogspot.com [accessed 30 June 2007 (translator)] for a list of Iraqi blogs.

52 See http://en.wikipedia.org/wiki/Iranian_Blogs [accessed 30 June 2007 (translator)] for a list of Iranian blogs.

Conclusion

Having reached this point I could limit myself to writing: and that's all. Or at least that the chapters that have gone before have covered all that I have to say about what I discovered in the course of my inquiry into the 'dark side' of the World Wide Web. But would that be really true? In a certain sense, yes. I set myself the task of documenting how the web is crowded with sites which, though with differing linguistic codes and with different levels of intensity and effectiveness, liberally dish out hate – something that not everyone, perhaps, is aware of – and I hope that I have been able to do so in a way that is convincing, while at the same time showing how these presences are neither sporadic nor constitute hidden niches only capable of attracting the attention of a miserable handful of visitors. The picture that emerges should be sufficient to demonstrate how the Internet, a means of communication which, thanks to the freedom that if offers, permits everyone to express their opinion, can have the undesirable consequence of also giving voice to very crude languages which sometimes even extol recourse to physical violence and war.

All the textbooks on communication tell us that thanks to the Internet we are no longer relegated to the simple role of users of prepackaged information content but that each one of us can ourselves become producers of communication. All you need is a computer, an Internet connection and a server that will host what we think will immediately become accessible to an audience of millions. This book, I believe, is the umpteenth confirmation of this. That all of this brings us to ask ourselves whether what we deem unacceptable content still has a right to be expressed, or whether what we judge to be a distorted use of the web should be in some way the object of restrictive measures, seems to me a development that is as inevitable – and legitimate – as it is lazy. By its very nature it is not possible to censor or black out a website. Or, rather, it is technically possible in the short term by obliging the provider hosting the site to cancel it from its server, but if they want to keep it alive its managers need only find a different provider, perhaps in a more compliant country, and in a day or two they will be able to resuscitate the site without too much difficulty. I have already mentioned this phenomenon with regard to the websites of armed Middle-Eastern groups.

Hosted for a time in Malaysia,[1] when the Malaysian government forced their providers to close them down because of Western pressure, all they did was shift their operations elsewhere, some to Middle-Eastern countries, others to Europe and still others, ironically, to the United States.[2]

If I may express an opinion on this question, it seems to me that though the difficulty of censoring or limiting communication via computer may be unwelcome, we might as well exploit the advantages which derive from it. Advantages which are far from negligible and which concern the possibility of personal access, without the filter of intermediaries, to points of view and experiences beyond those which form part of our world of knowledge, though exposure to such messages may increase our fears and anxieties. In short I share the opinion of Cass Sunstein and what he says in his book *Republic.com*.[3] According to Sunstein, in an epoch in which most communications make use of telecommunications networks and in which the number of information sources are consequently increasing exponentially, there is a serious risk of a hardening tendency to select the information we want to receive on the basis of conformity with the convictions we have already acquired.

In other words, it is easy to fall prey to the temptation of erecting walls about our universe of communication so that we only receive news that interests us and we exclude *a priori* anything that does not correspond to our tastes or to our beliefs. Yet exposure to material that we have not pre-selected, and which we would rather not encounter, is an important requisite for the creation of a more balanced view of the world in which we live and of its problems since it increases our chances of getting an idea, however limited, of the arguments sustained by those who have a different – sometimes a radically different – opinion to our own.

Today, thanks to our information technologies and the services offered by numerous dotcoms, we can make a sort of 'Daily Me' appear on the screen of our computer or our cell phone – a daily news page cut to our own personal measure, whose contents reflect our deepest convictions – but Sunstein insists that it is imperative that we go in the opposite direction and open up to communicative encounters which are not planned or predictable,

---

1   See the CD-ROM 'Digital Terrorism and Hate 2003' published by the Simon Wiesenthal Centre.

2   See the almost daily reports which appear on the Internet Haganah site. I remember, in this regard, the answer given by an American provider to a letter of protest from Aaron Weisburd – who runs Internet Haganah – and which Weisburd published on his site. It was of this tone: 'These clients have regularly paid our fees and have accepted our conditions: not to publish obscene or pedophilic material. If you believe they have broken the law, report them to the American authorities and in the event that they are told to close we will take appropriate measures'. Unfortunately I didn't record the name of the site in question.

3   Sunstein, C. (2002) *Republic.com* (Princeton University Press).

thus avoiding the danger, in a society already strongly fragmented like our own, of finding ourselves entrapped in a communicative universe in which we can only hear the echo of our own voice, or that of those who think like us. Listening to the opinions of those with whom we don't agree certainly involves discomfort, irritation and even disgust, but only in this way will it be possible to create a general awareness of the problems we face and to break our habit of relying on one-eyed modes of thought. In any event, the result would inevitably be an enrichment of our awareness, and more information would be brought into circulation than is currently offered on a daily basis by the great communication conglomerates.

At the same time, however, I do not believe that the existence of hate sites is a problem that can be reduced to a matter of acknowledging their existence and treating them as source of broader awareness. We must honestly face up to the fact that behind these sites there are real movements and groups whose *raison d'être* derives from their separateness and their opposition to, and rejection of, civil processes of problem resolution. It is not that their voices are discordant or that despite using a language that is all their own they really want, deep down, to be heard and to claim rights of citizenship on an equal basis. These sites speak for groups and movements composed of men and women of flesh and blood who have substituted the word war – it little matters whether symbolically or in real terms – for that of dialogue and have constructed their identities and their mode of confronting the rest of the world on this basis. They use the Internet as a meeting place, as a place to exchange information and to reciprocally stoke their own passions. Above all they use the Internet to create fences, put up barriers and dig defensive ditches between those who are with them and those who are against them. But if the Internet facilitates communication between these groups and movements it also shows us that they have attained, through growth and consolidation, what can be undoubtedly be described as a critical mass. I repeat: it does not seem to me that these groups are marginal, nor that their existence is a precarious one. On the contrary, the Internet has revealed that they are strongly rooted on the web, active on the level of communication at a distance and numerically substantial. And I fear, in constant growth. In short, this new technology has provided a home for a growing archipelago, consisting of islands Balkanized according to precise membership criteria, which look upon those who surround them with such scorn and intolerance that they define them as enemies against whom to wage a war that gives no quarter.

Agreed, the examples which I have offered are extreme and might be considered lacking in general significance. Has the world – it might be objected – ever been a completely peaceful place? When did there ever exist a world formed of a plurality of cultures and communities which respected each others' reciprocal differences and lived together in mutual tolerance? True. But in that case we also have to admit that the facts tell us that the immanent Internet of which Barry Wellman[4] talks has not changed things much. Indeed, that it has had the opposite effect. Until a short time ago there were those who argued that a revolutionary technology like the Internet would be able to produce significant social innovations, and would even be able to modify existing equilibriums at world level in favour of a more globalized society that could break down barriers and fences, renew local traditions and contribute to the bridging of the many divides which still afflict important parts of our planet.[5] It seems to me that the examples that I have offered confirm instead that it is not technological innovation in itself that produces change but if anything the use that is made of it. In fact, technologies are never adopted as their inventors intend but are always adapted, by those who use them, to their own needs, their own interests and their own objectives. In the case of the Internet this technology permits us, for example, to widen our range of social relations by enabling us to keep in daily contact with people on the other side of the Atlantic thanks to email, Webcams or VOIP.[6] It can give a voice to those who have something interesting to say but who in the absence of the Internet would be at a loss for means to express it. Voices which can become authoritative and win the attention of a vast audience. As is the case with blogs and more recently with podcasting.[7]

But what has also happened, as we have seen, is that the Internet has become a means by which old resentments draw new breath, contempt for the other is manifested in all its virulence, hate for who is on the other side is screamed with words dripping in blood, and the desire to settle old scores is exhibited brandishing the most menacing of symbols. Thus the Internet shows us, as in a mirror, how the difficult road towards societies that are peaceful and tolerant comes up against the obstacle of ancient forms of rivalry, both within our own social systems and beyond their boundaries. Those rivalries between groups, races and cultures which occupy the historical stage and which have seized on and found new vigour in the most modern of technologies.

---

4   Wellman, B. and Hogan, B., *The Immanent Internet.*

5   This view amounts to 'technological determinism'. On this see Bourdon, J. (2001) Introduzione ai media, trad. it. (Bologna: Il Mulino), p. 31 and foll.

6   VOIP is an acronym of Voice over IP and refers to the use of the Internet for making phone calls. See http://en.wikipedia.org/wiki/VoIP.

7   Podcasting is a new form of communication via computer which consists in the production and posting on line of transmissions – called podcasts – of various kinds, from music to news programs. These files can be downloaded and transferred to an MP3 player. In Italy, Radio Vaticana was one of the first to use podcasting.

If this is true, then it seems questionable whether the Internet can, by itself, open up a road free of obstacles which can take us towards a global village in which every citizen will be permeated by cosmopolitanism, universalism and egalitarianism. Rather, it pins us down, through the multiplicity of languages to which it permits expression, before an incommunicability between conflicting social galaxies that it will take a long time to overcome and transform – or at least this is what I hope – into interaction between systems of different values. The effort required does not have its best weapon in the variegated world of pixels but rather in the capacity of many to overcome the auto-referential forms of communication that still divide us and find a new real communal space.

Index

Advances in Criminology

Full series list